THE ESSEX BED-SIDE BOOK

LONDON BOROUGH OF LEWISHAM
LIBRARY SERVICE

Author

Title

Books or discs must be returned on or before the last date stamped on label or on card in book pocket. Books or discs can be renewed by telephone, letter or personal call unless required by another reader. After library hours use the Ansafone Service (01-698 7347). For hours of opening and charges see notices at the above branch, but note that all lending departments close at 1 pm on Wednesday and all libraries are closed on Sundays, Good Friday, Christmas Day, Bank Holidays and Saturdays prior to Bank Holidays.

THE ESSEX BED-SIDE BOOK

An anthology in words and pictures for lovers of the Essex countryside

Compiled by
F. G. Whitnall

Published by
ESSEX COUNTRYSIDE
LETCHWORTH PRINTERS LTD.
NORTON WAY NORTH
LETCHWORTH
HERTS

Printed by Letchworth Printers Ltd.,
Norton Way North, Letchworth, Herts

ACKNOWLEDGMENTS

"Essex Ancient and Modern," from *Colourful Britain*, published by Jarrold and Sons Ltd.

"Beyond the Fringe," from *Rambles in Essex*, published by British Rail.

"Enchanting Country," from *The Last Stronghold of Sail*, published by George G. Harrap and Co. Ltd.

"A Question of Taste," from *Vision of England—Kent and Essex*, published by Elek Books Ltd.

"A Land of Birds and Drifting Fogs," from *The Coast of Enchanted Wings*, published by Blandford Press.

"Treasury of Beauty," from *The Last Stronghold of Sail*, published by George G. Harrap and Co. Ltd.

"The Age-old Enemy," from *The Great Tide*, published by Essex County Council.

"Captains Courageous," from *Discovering the Essex Coast*, published by Essex Countryside.

"The East Coast Packet," from *Once Upon a Tide*, published by George G. Harrap and Co. Ltd., 1955.

"Those Lovely, Lovely Curves," from *Tideways and Byways of Essex and Suffolk*, published by Edward Arnold and Co.

"Still a World of Sail," from *Coasting Bargemaster*, published by Edward Arnold and Co.

"A Wet Shirt and an 'appy 'eart," from *Down Tops'l*, published by George G. Harrap and Co. Ltd.

"The Salt of the Earth," from *The Coast of Enchanted Wings*, published by Blandford Press.

"Tyburn Dick," from *The Lords-Lieutenants and Keepers of the Rolls of The County of Essex*, printed by Whitehead-Morris Ltd.

"Gammer Miggs," from *Dear Countrymen*, published by Gerald Duckworth and Co. Ltd.

"Old Dummy," from *Highways and Byways in Essex*, published by Macmillan and Co. Ltd.

"Father William," from *A Marshland Omnibus*, published by Gerald Duckworth and Co. Ltd.

"Old Syd," from *Essex Countryside.*

"Proud Pedigree," from *Heraldry in Essex*, published by Essex County Council.

"A Cottage in the Country," from *Essex Countryside.*

"To Stew Carps," from *English History from Essex Sources*, published by Essex County Council.

"Pork Plugga—an Essex Speciality," from *Country Dishes*, published by Longacre Press Ltd.

"Learn and Inwardly Digest," from *English History from Essex Sources 1750-1900*, published by Essex County Council.

"Education: Tuppence a Week," from *Essex Countryside.*

"These New-fangled Ways," from *Essex Ballads,* published by Benham Newspapers Ltd.

"Teacher—at ten bob a month—nearly," from *Essex Countyside.*

"Corporal Punishment," from *Essex Schooldays,* published by Hutchinson and Co. Ltd.

"The Girls of St. Monica's," from *Essex Countryside.*

"Dear Sir . . .," from *Essex Countryside.*

"Harvest Time," from *An Essex Harvest,* published by Chatto and Windus Ltd.

"Lot No. 121—What am I bid?" from *Overheard in the Essex Country in the Early 90s,* published by Arthur Stockwell Ltd.

"Be Prepared," from *The Fire Office,* published by the Essex and Suffolk Equitable Insurance Society Ltd.

"Royal Fighting Talk," from *Royalty in Essex,* published by Essex County Council.

"The Manner of Handling Arms," from *English History from Essex Sources 1550-1750,* published by Essex County Council.

"That Sweet Enemy France," from *The Lords-Lieutenants and Keepers of the Rolls of the County of Essex,* printed by Whitehead Morris Ltd.

"The Lion's Roar," from *The Zeppelin Fighters,* published by Robert Hale Ltd.

"A Select Lot," from *With the 10th Essex in France,* published by Gay and Hancock Ltd.

"Over the Top! 1916," from *With the 10th Essex in France,* published by Gay and Hancock Ltd.

"Maldon Expects . . .," from *Warmen Courageous,* published by John H. Burrows and Sons Ltd.

"Enemy Raiders Approaching," from *The Oaken Heart,* published by Hutchinson and Co. Ltd.

"Home Guard," from *Warmen Courageous,* published by John H. Burrows and Sons Ltd.

"Thames-side Guardians," from *Coastal Adventure,* published by George G. Harrap and Co. Ltd.

"1941—An Eventful Year," from *Essex at War,* published by Benham and Co. Ltd.

"Orders is Orders," from *The Essex Regiment 1929-50,* published by the Essex Regiment Association.

"Of Rogues and Vagabonds," from *The Hundred of Beacontree—A Police Division of Essex,* published by J. C. Phelp and Son.

"The Moat Farm Murder," from *Highways and Byways in Essex,* published by Macmillan and Co. Ltd.

"The Card," from *Essex Blood and Thunder,* published by George Caunt.

"The Night Mail—1818," from *Highways and Byways of Essex,* published by Essex County Council.

"The Colchester Machine," from *Essex at Work 1700-1815,* published by Essex County Council.

"Bull-baiting," from *Highways and Byways in Essex,* published by Macmillan and Co. Ltd.

"Bent Caunt's Last Fight," from *Essex Blood and Thunder,* published by George Caunt.

"Wild-fowler," from *The Gun on Saltings and Stubble,* published by Herbert Jenkins Ltd.

"Goin' Fishin'," from *The Last Stronghald of Sail,* published by George G. Harrap and Co. Ltd.

"Village Cricket," from *The Oaken Heart,* published by Hutchinson and Co. Ltd.

"A Foreigner Remembers," from *Essex at Work 1700-1815,* published by Essex County Council.

"Christmas Supper at the Wheatsheaf," from *Essex Folk,* published by Heath Cranton Ltd.

"Christmas Day in the Workhouse," from *The Essex Standard.*

"Harvest Supper," from *Essex Folk,* published by Heath Cranton Ltd.

"The Sunday School Treat," from *Essex Folk,* published by Heath Cranton Ltd.

"A Poacher's Wedding," from *A Poacher's Tale,* published by G. Bell and Sons Ltd.

"Christianity Comes to Essex," from *A History of the English Church and People,* published by Penguin Books Ltd.

"A Reg'lar Bad 'Un," from *Essex Folk,* published by Heath Cranton Ltd.

"The Preaching will go on," from *Men of Vision* (no publisher given).

"Mrs. Cope's 'Essence of Vipers,'" from *English History from Essex Sources 1550-1750,* published by Essex County Council.

"The Snail Gruel for Consumption," from *English History from Essex Sources 1550-1750,* published by Essex County Council.

"Dr. Daffy's Elixir," from *Essex Countryside.*

"A Certain Cure for Earache," from *Essex Countryside.*

"End of a Fiery Monster," from *Essex Pie,* published by Benham and Co. Ltd.

"Of Ghoulies and Ghosties," from *Haunted Borley* (no publisher given).

CONTENTS

Section

FRONTISNOTE

". . . of all the counties of England, the one of which the least is known by English people generally is the county of Essex. It has been given a bad name as a flat county, an uninteresting county, an anguish county, a county without society, a hopelessly unresidential county; in fact, so many bad names have been bestowed upon it that it has been hanged over and over again, and may be reckoned as a dead county. Yet there is a great deal of life actually remaining in Essex, and life, too, which is not without attractiveness for those who will take the trouble to study it . . ."

From *John Lott's Alice*
by Frances G. Burmester.

INTRODUCTION

In recent years there has been a marked increase in the numbers of people wishing to know more about Essex—still the fifth largest administrative county in England in terms of population and the twelfth largest in terms of area.

The story of the county has to be searched for. Not only on foot, in a motor car or at extra-mural classes, but also among the numerous hand-written and printed sources of material made available to the public over the years.

In compiling this anthology my purpose has been to use some of the lesser-known sources which record the commonplace as well as the legendary. Understandably, any anthology cannot include every item one would like but it is hoped that this miscellany might tempt the reader to begin or continue an individual search of a county whose story excites both the imagination and the intellect: a story which rarely fails to interest or entertain.

I wish to thank the many writers whose work is represented in this volume; also Mr. Peter Henderson and the staff of the Essex county library service for their invaluable help in supplying many of the original sources. Thanks also to my wife, who in spite of a thousand and one other things to attend to has helped me mother this particular infant from start to finish.

Section 1

IN PRAISE OF ESSEX

ESSEX—ANCIENT AND MODERN

MANY counties in England are like the hymns, both ancient and modern, none more so than Essex, so called because it was the land of the East Saxons. Where it touches London, there are great modern factories and docks, and some new towns have been built within its boundaries; at other points it seems to have been little touched by the passage of the years . . .

From *Colourful Britain*
by Robert Kemp, 1967.

IN PRAISE OF ESSEX

THIS shire is moste fatt, frutefull, and full of profitable thinges, exceding (as farr as I can finde) anie other shire, for the generall comodeties . . . this shire seemeth to me to deserve the title of the englishe Goshen, (place of light and plenty) the fattest of the Lande: comparable to Palestina, that flowed with milke and hunnye. But I can not comende the healthfulness of it: And especiallie nere the sea coastes, Rochford, Denge, Tendering hundredes and other lowe places about the creekes, which gave me a moste cruell quarterne fever. But the manie and sweete comodeties countervayle the daunger . . . This shire is well planted with noblemen and gentlemen, as also not a few sufficient and able yeomen . . .

From *Description of Essex*
by John Norden, 1594.

BEYOND THE FRINGE

In the main, Essex is hilly, well-wooded and full of beauty and interest. The general ignorance on these points is based on the fact that the county has been little explored by the tourist. The best-known sections of it lie along the Thames estuary, which, of course, is decidedly flat, and up the valley of the river Lea, which runs through a level and industrial district. But these are only the faded fringes on a gracious garment, clothing a green and beautiful countryside.

From *Rambles in Essex*

by Pathfinder, 1950.

RICH IN THE ANCIENT ART

Few districts offer subjects of higher interest; and although I must admit the want of the beauties of a stately cathedral, yet it remains of Roman castrametation—its castellated and its monastic ruins—its ecclesiastical and domestic structures—present, in singularity of design and construction, unparalleled examples of ancient art. The Roman works at Chesterford, considered by some as the most entire in England; the castles of Colchester and Hedingham; the Abbey of Waltham and the Priory of St. Botolph, both exceedingly curious specimens; the round church of Maplested; and above all, the wooden church of Greensted, perhaps a genuine instance of Anglo-Saxon Architecture; the houses of Layer Marney and Audley-end, these, and various others that might be justly adduced, will, I think, bear me out in asserting that the county of Essex is not to be surpassed in the possession of those curious and interesting remains which constitute the riches of architectural antiquities.

From *Memorials of the Antiquities . . . of Essex*

by Alfred Suckling, 1845.

PURSUIT OF SWEETNESS

NINE people out of ten are struck with amazement when you speak of Essex as a holiday field. They imagine it is an utter abomination of desolation. It is an article of faith with many that there are no hills in Essex. With those who know better, this assertion only provokes a smile; but, as happens with most vulgar errors, it dies hard. Like the primal curse pronounced upon man, it can only be expiated by the sweat of his brow. It is true that other parts of England can show bolder heights, lovelier rivers, more opulent architecture than Essex; but for variety of interest, and for a certain homelike sweetness which excites not only admiration but affection, Essex bears the palm.

From *Romantic Essex*
by Reginald A. Beckett, 1901.

IF I WERE TO OWN . . .

IF I were to own this countryside
As far as a man in a day could ride,
And the Tyes were mine for giving or letting,—
Wingle Tye and Margaretting
Tye,—and Skreens, Gooshays, and Cockerells,
Shellow, Rochetts, Bandish and Pickerells,
Martins, Lambkins, and Lillyputs,
Their copses, ponds, roads and ruts,
Fields where plough horses steam and plovers
Fling and Whimper, hedges that lovers
Love, and orchards, shrubberies, walls
Where the sun untroubled by north wind falls,
And single trees where the thrush sings well
His proverbs untranslatable,
I would give them all to my son
If he would let me any one
For a song, a blackbird's song, at dawn.
He should have no more, till on my lawn
Never a one was left, because I

Had shot them to put them into a pie,—
His Essex blackbirds, every one,
And I was left old and alone.
Then unless I could pay, for rent, a song
As sweet as a blackbird's, and as long—
No more—he should have the house, not I
Margaretting or Wingle Tye,
Or it might be Skreens, Gooshays, or Cockerells,
Shellow, Rochetts, Bandish or Pickerells,
Martins, Lambkins, or Lillyputs,
Should be his till the cart tracks had no ruts.

From *Collected Poems*
by Edward Thomas (1877-1917).

ENCHANTING COUNTRY

THE map of the east coast of England shows quite an appreciable nick between Harwich and the Thames . . .

It is enchanting and enchanted country. On a brisk June morning the great heaped white clouds go sweeping across the wide skies, and the peewits wheel below them; a summer afternoon finds the floodtide rippling and searching among marshes shimmering with that most exquisite of carpets, the mauve-tinted sea-lavender; at evening the descending sun casts a spell over the moisture-laden waters and sends land merging into sea and bathes it all with rose, pearl and gold; on a bitter winter's night the wild swans strain low over the creaking ice-floes, lit in weird, ghostly spasms as the ragged clouds race across the moon.

And through all its creeks and inlets the tides ebb and flow as they have since time began—through all the " bays, channels, roads, bars, strands, harbours, havens, rivers, streams, creeks, and places within the said limits contained," as the old Customs records put it. They are the very pulse-beat of eternity, the tides, and to dwell awhile in a realm ruled by their unchanging, unhasting tempo guides the mind, uneasily attuned to the fevered rhythm of a modern world, into a contemplation of things wide and infinite, a sympathy with natural forces which is an experience as profound, stimulating, and satisfying as a man can know.

From *The Last Stronghold of Sail*
by Hervey Benham, 1948.

A QUESTION OF TASTE

" ESSEX must be viewed as a whole, warts and all, and nobody knows the warts better than the present writer."

J. G. O'Leary, Editor,
Essex Journal.

For almost half a century Essex has been accounted the poor relation amongst the English counties. Although a Home County comparatively few retiring or week-ending Londoners ever want to make a home in it; while on the other side of the map the people who live in East Anglia make it clear that Essex has no claim whatever to that distinctive title. It is at once too cockneyfied for the Londoners and too London for the real countryman—or so it would seem. " Not Essex! " plead the despairing househunters, advertising for a house anywhere in any condition at any price except for that one corner sinister. Liverpool Street doubtless looms before the traveller by train—a natural enough deterrent, while the motorist, faced with the frustrations and desolations of the East End, unless he travels circuitously by way of Epping, usually prefers to turn elsewhere.

It is natural enough, and yet it was not always so. And that it is so now is, oddly enough, one reason why so much of Essex still retains its own county character—unspoiled because, in the opinion of so many, it is already spoiled beyond hope.

Besides, truth to tell, Essex went out of fashion as a place to live in after the days of the Tudors, and to be out of fashion is to suffer a worse fate than to bear the reputation of flatness or to come and go through the grimy portals of Liverpool Street Station.

Fundamentally, however, one comes down to the question of taste. There are people who like to live in a "coming" place and others who like to live in a going one—or, better still, a gone.

From *Vision of England—Kent-Essex*
by Reginald Turnor and Phoebe
Fenwick Gaye, 1956.

A YACHTSMAN'S PARADISE

In Essex there is greater tranquillity if less conspicuous beauty. The water-ways are more diversified, go farther into the land, and offer more unusual aspects than the Medway, the only really navigable river on the north shore. Essex is, comparatively, an unknown land. Its quiet beauties and splendid views have not often been sung. Everyone hears of the gardens of Kent, the downs of Sussex, the heaths and forests of Hampshire, the combes of Dorsetshire, the lanes of Devon, and the tors of Cornwall; but Essex is known only for its marshes. How has this libellous idea got abroad? Certainly it only dates from modern times. In the days of the Plantagenets and the Tudors it was the fashionable, the court county.

Few counties have finer manor houses, more magnificent monumental tombs, timber work of a nobler architectural character, than Essex. The country is hilly in many parts. The views from the Laindon Hills, Hadleigh Castle, Danbury Church, Ashingdon and Great Totham have a beauty and extent all their own. There is fishing in all the creeks, and sport of every kind ashore . . . all we have to do is to show what a really delightful cruising-ground there is within an hour or two of London, with much of the interest of Holland, and the quiet seclusion of Devonshire.

For people engaged in the City the advantages are very great, owing to the perfect safety with which a boat can be left anywhere in the creeks, while the owner runs up to town at the cost of an hour-and-a-half at most.

From *Sailing Tours*
by Frank Cowper, 1892.

ESSEX

I go through the fields of blue water
  On the south road of the sea:
High to north, the East country
  Holds her green fields to me,
For she that I gave over
  Gives not over me.

Last night I lay at Good Easter
  Under a hedge I knew;
Last night in wood by High Easter
  I trod the May-floors blue:
Out of the sea the sun came
  Bidding me wake and rue.

Roding, that names eight churches
  (Banks with the paigles pight),
Chelmer, whose mill and willows
  Keep one red tower in sight,
Under the Southern Cross run
  Beside our ship to-night.

Ah! I may not go back now,
  Neither be turned nor stayed,
Yet should I live, I'd seek her,
  Once that my vows are paid,
And should I die, I'd haunt her,
  I being what God made.

England has greater counties,
  Their peace to hers is small.
Low hills, rich fields, calm rivers!
  In Essex, seek them all—
Essex, where I that found them
  Did but lose them all!

Arthur Shearley Cripps, 1906.

Section 2

THE GOOD EARTH

OF PROVERBIAL GOODNESS

THE divisions of Essex are twofold, natural and artificial; the first consisting of continent and islands; the latter of hundreds, towns, parishes and hamlets. The islands border partly upon the German ocean, and partly on the Thames. One peculiarity of the county is, that with Suffolk and Norfolk it forms the largest connected space of level ground in the whole island. Its surface, however, is not wholly flat, but has many gentle hills and dales . . . Agriculture, which has much improved the face of the county, is the principal feature of it, the produce of which consists of live stock, chiefly calves (for their goodness Essex has long been proverbial), besides the finest wheat and all other kinds of grain and hops, coriander, caraway, saffron, teazle, etc.

From *Excursions in the County of Essex*
by P. Youngman, 1818.

A PRECIOUS GIFT

IF I should ever by chance grow rich
I'll buy Codham, Cockridden, and Childerditch,
Roses, Pyrgo, and Lapwater,
And let them all to my elder daughter.
The rent I shall ask of her will be only
Each year's first violets, white and lovely,
The first primroses and orchises—
She must find them before I do, that is.
But if she finds a blossom on furze

Without rent they shall all for ever be hers,
Whenever I am sufficiently rich:
Codham, Cockridden, and Childerditch,
Roses, Pyrgo and Lapwater,—
I shall give them all to my elder daughter.

From *Collected Poems*
by Edward Thomas (1877-1917).

BOUNTEOUS EARTH

ESSEX does not, indeed, present the picturesque beauty of the west, and the bold contour of some of the northern counties; neither does it fatigue the sight with the almost unvarying flatness and uniformity of Cambridgeshire and Huntingdonshire. There is no rude mountain or barren crag to give what has been called " the charm of desolation " to the scene. There is scarcely an acre, save of its forest lands on the north and west, and a few scattered commons . . . that has not been rendered productive.

From *The People's History of Essex*
by D. W. Coller, 1861.

A LAND OF BIRDS AND DRIFTING FOGS

EAST Essex is again as it was and always will be—a land of birds and drifting fogs and bitter winds and the loneliness which is near to God . . .

It is a coast for the naturalist and the wildfowler, the man who loves the solitude of a small boat in a silent creek.

The space of immense levels and high skies. The purple and silver of mud-flat, the glitter and sheen of creeping tide, the drift of suaeda pods on summer water; and the sea-wind running like mice through summer singing grasses; the clang and whistle of wildfowl and waders; the croak of geese in the winter dawns and drift of herons at snowy eve. These are the sounds and colours of this land. A roadless land and a houseless land. Down on the marshes the only roads are still the old, green, barge roads, those raised and silent trackways which run from upland farm lanes where straw hangs on the hedges and finches scold the weasel, to the hairy sea-walls where, on the creek-edge, the black piles of an ancient and disused staithe mark where once the barges lay days and nights on end while wheat was loaded or cattle were driven aboard for transport to the mainland.

From *The Coast of Enchanted Wings*
by J. Wentworth Day, 1946.

MISTY MOON MARSH

WHERE is Misty Moon Marsh?

It lies somewhere in that ' recondite region ' bounded by the Stour and Lower Hope Reach on the Thames . . .

At the quiet village which overhangs the winding creek intersecting the salt marshes nothing seems doing, for the tide is out and does not ' serve'. A few boats and craft of the humbler sort lie canted on the mud bordering the attenuated ribbon of water, tributaries of which form mooring-places for two or three house-barges. The approach to these habitations is invariably in the form of a quaint little gang-way, terminating in a drawbridge some four feet in length. Farther on the tributary squeezes out into a sort of ditch or moat, replete with disused kettles and broken pans. On an eminence near by the square tower of the church dominates the sun-drenched village street, with its tumbled group of picturesque sixteenth-century houses . . . There is a hospitable-looking big-beamed old inn, full of quaint nooks and unexpected corners, where homely fare is served by a comely damsel . . .

Beyond the creek and stretching out interminably beneath the river-wall that skirts it lies the marsh, shimmering and vibrating in the heat like a mirage seen through a veil of vapour. A few ruminating cattle and hoarse, soaring sea-gulls are almost the only living things in sight. Myriads of insects hum out a monotonous cadence. Stranded on the mud in the distance is a good-sized barge with its sails clewed up, and apparently tenantless. Farther away still on the sea-wall lies the inert carcass of a wreck. From the river-wall bordering the creek some rickety wooden steps descend to the sun-fissured flats, and rotten little timber bridges here and there traverse the ' rhines ', as they are often called—or used to be—in this part of the country . . . Evening comes on, and the sun goes down in a stormy rent of fiery clouds. A chill breath from across the water makes itself felt, with a suspicion of wind-haze . . . behind us a faint, mysterious radiance over the higher ground indicates that the moon is rising. An owl is hooting somewhere, and ruddy lights appear in the windows of the inn, from whence snatches of a bacchanalian song emerge on the opening of the tap-room door.

From *Essex Survivals*
by Fred Roe, 1929.

TREASURY OF BEAUTY

SALCOT Creek, winding away to where the unspoiled twin hamlets of Salcot and Virley are linked across it by a little bridge, is a perfect example of the charm of the Essex marshlands, and Tollesbury Creek weaves tortuously inland to provide an unexpected arrival at a thriving little yachting centre, with twelve-metres and big schooners and power yachts hauled up in winter on the slipways of its yards. At low water the creek dwindles to a trickle, and one wonders how ever they got there.

Such is the Blackwater, treasury of beauty and of history of every kind.

From *The Last Stronghold of Sail*
by Hervey Benham, 1948.

SUNBURST

THE light wheels and comes in
over the seawall
and the bitter turf
that not only wind has scathed but
all this wheeling and flashing, this
sunburst comes across us.

At Holland on Sea
at an angle from here and
some miles distant
a fisherman reels back blinded,
a walker is sliced in two.
The silver disc came at them
edgewise, seconds ago.

Light that robes us, does it?
Limply, as robes do, moulded
to the frame of Nature? It
has no furious virtue?

From *Essex Poems* (1963-67)
by Donald Davie.

EPPING FOREST

THE forest is like the sea . . . its moods are many; they are never quite the same; and one never tires of it . . .

From *All in a Garden Fair*
by Walter Besant.

UNDER THE GREENWOOD TREE

MORE than once, on cloudy days, I have found myself quite lost among the trees, without the least notion of the points of the compass. But nowhere is it a gloomy forest (Epping Forest), owing perhaps to the marked absence of pines and firs; in fact, the woodland is thoroughly English. The paths take one up and down steep declivities, through swampy hollows, across little streamlets running silently over beds of decaying leaves. In the seasons when the forest is least frequented it is also the most beautiful. In spring the different greens of the various trees are wonderfully striking, from a point such as High Beech where a wide stretch of woodland can be seen. Even when the skies are dark with gathering snow a wonderful picture is presented by the wooded ridges, the nearer ones blended into a mass of sepia contrasting with the opal blue of the more distant. But the forest in autumn is most wonderful of all, when the russet and gold of the trees are bathed in the calm sunshine of Indian summer; the hillsides are clothed with purple heather, or with glowing masses of copper-coloured bracken; and the vivid green grass is sprinkled with fallen leaves of the brightest scarlet.

From *Romantic Essex*
by Reginald A. Beckett, 1901.

A ROYAL PREROGATIVE

KING Henry VIII is said to have preferred Epping to any other Royal Forest in England for hunting purposes. So fond was he of it that, according to an old tradition, he went to the hunt there on the morning that his Queen, Anne Boleyn, was executed, setting out the moment he heard a signal gun which told him that the fatal deed was done.

From *Bygone Essex*
by William Andrews, 1892.

Section 3

SEA, SHIPS AND SAILOR-MEN

THE AGE-OLD ENEMY

ESSEX and the sea have been antagonists for centuries. ' On the east ', wrote John Norden, the Elizabethan topographer, Essex ' encountreth the mayne Ocean, an infallable bounde '. Ceaselessly the conflict born of that encounter flows backwards and forwards with the tide. The creeks, estuaries and rivers of the Essex coast—Stour and Colne, Blackwater, Crouch and Roach, Thames, Ingrebourne, Roding and Lea—are arms of the sea restlessly probing the heart of the county . . .

Today the county is a walled fortress. More than three hundred miles of man-made defences barricade its flat marshland borders against the thrusting tide outside. If the walls were not there, much of the land they protect would be claimed by the sea, for it lies below high water mark. The walls run in almost unbroken sequence, from the muddy saltings of Judas Gap, at the head of the Stour estuary, right round to the wharves, warehouses and docks of the Port of London. They front the open sea boldly, and wind interminably round the creeks, only interrupted, here and there, by a short stretch of clay cliff, a quay, ' hard ', wharf or seaside promenade, or, on Thames-side, a plateau of refuse ' tipped ' on the marshland and itself part of the defensive system.

More than eight hundred years of effort lie behind the present defences. They are a monument to human perseverance.

From *The Great Tide*
by Hilda Grieve, 1959.

THIS GREY SEAWAY OF OURS

UPON those big maps of our school-days, all the sea was painted alike one uniform and generous blue. But the yachtsman who sets sail from Brightlingsea, trusting to that blue-water theory of the school-room, will not long await his moment of disillusion . . .

The great wilderness of sands and banks, pierced only by narrow fairways, is reputed to have rendered this corner of coast one of the most dangerous coasts in the world. If an imaginary line be drawn from the North Foreland in Kent to Orfordness in Suffolk, the whole of the sea thus enclosed is shoal and sandbank, and its only deep-water channels are those kept open by the scour of the tide in and out of the rivers. All the rest is treacherous shoalwater, a death-trap for unwary ships. These sands teem with the ribs of them.

Following the tidal currents that set in and out of the Thames, the sandbanks run out like long fingers north-eastward from the Nore—the Barrow Sand, Sunk Sand, Long Sand and so on—and the narrow fairways make landward between them. The great channels lead into the Thames, while minor fairways give access to the Crouch, Colne and Blackwater.

This then is that shoal-riddled grey seaway of ours, over the grey distances of which the sea-borne traffic of the ancient London has searched its careful way for centuries.

From *Shoalwater and Fairway*
by H. Alker Tripp, 1924.

THE NORE LIGHT

" THE Nore Light " is a great strong vessel painted red, with the name in white letters, some six or seven feet high, along her side. Her mast stands in the middle of the ship, surmounted by a red ball and a big lantern, with the machinery for the revolving light built round the mast. At night this is hove up to the hounds. A wonderful ray it sends quivering round the horizon, lighting up for a moment the passing ships, which appear like ghosts and vanish. A horn is sounded in foggy weather, and a gun is fired when vessels are seen to be standing into danger. The sand-bank of which it marks the eastern end stretches away to the west, nearly up to Yantlet Creek.

From *London to the Nore*
by W. L. and M. A. Wyllie, 1905.

UPON THE WATERS DARK AND RUDE

ON Saturday sailed from Bremen,
American-outward-bound,
Take settler and seamen, tell men with women,
Two hundred souls in the round—
O Father, not under thy feathers nor ever as guessing
The goal was a shoal, of a fourth the doom to be drowned;
Yet did the dark side of the bay of thy blessing
Not vault them, the millions of rounds of thy mercy not reeve even them in?

Into the snows she sweeps,
Hurling the haven behind,
The DEUTSCHLAND, on Sunday; and so the sky keeps,
For the infinite air is unkind,
And the sea flint-flake, black-backed in the regular blow,
Sitting Eastnortheast, in cursed quarter, the wind;
Wiry and white-fiery and whirlwind-swivelled snow
Spins to the widow-making unchilding unfathering deeps.

She drove in the dark to leeward,
She struck—not a reef or a rock
But the combs of a smother of sand: night drew her
Dead to the Kentish Knock;
And she beat the bank down with her bows and the ride of her keel:
The breakers rolled on her beam with ruinous shock;
And canvas and compass, the whorl and the wheel
Idle for ever to waft her or wind her with, these she endured.

Hope had grown grey hairs,
Hope had mourning on,
Trenched with tears, carved with cares,
Hope was twelve hours gone;
And frightful a nightfall folded rueful a day
Nor rescue, only rocket and lightship, shone,
And lives at last were washing away:
To the shrouds they took,—they shook in the hurling and horrible airs.

One stirred from the rigging to save
The wild woman-kind below,
With a rope's end round the man, handy and brave—
He was pitched to his death at a blow,
For all his dreadnought breast and braids of thew:
They could tell him for hours, dandled the to and fro
Through the cobbled foam-fleece, what could he do
With the burl of the fountains of air, buck and the flood of the wave?

They fought with God's cold—
And they could not and fell to the deck
(Crushed them) or water (and drowned them) or rolled
With the sea-romp over the wreck.
Night roared, with the heart-break hearing a heart-broke rabble,
The woman's wailing, the crying of child without check—
Till a lioness arose breasting the babble,
A prophetess towered in the tumult, a virginal tongue told.

From *The Wreck of the Deutschland*
by Gerard Manley Hopkins (1844-89).

TO THE RESCUE

SNOW-CLOUDS filled the sky when the little billy-boy ketch *DAYS* left London on Christmas Eve 1890, with a cargo of scrap-iron for Sunderland. On board were her owner-skipper, Henry Sweeting, the mate, Edward Hamilton, and a seventeen-year-old boy, George Lewington, who had bade his parents farewell and left his home at Grays not long before.

She sheltered from the weather for several days off Southend, leaving there on January 5th, 1891, to make her way slowly along the Essex coast against the bitter, snow-laden wind. Midnight found her off Harwich, and in the early morning, struggling through a blinding snowstorm, she struck on the Cork Sand.

The skipper rushed forward with a lead line. Five fathoms . . . He cast the lead again. Eight fathoms . . .

The worst is over he thought. But a minute or two later there was a crash as she struck heavily on another part of the sand, and when the skipper dashed below to get a light he found himself up to the waist in water. He and his two companions tried to launch their small boat, but the waves caught it and smashed it against the billy-boy's side and stove it in. As the wreckage of the little boat was carried away by the swirling waves the ketch sank beneath them. All three climbed into the port rigging, the skipper lashing the youngster near him so that he could lean over and try and warm him by rubbing his face and hands.

'George, keep up lad, the lifeboat's coming,' the skipper told him. But no lifeboat came, and after they had clung to the rigging for five long agonising hours the boy died. It was not until dawn that the light-keepers aboard the Cork lightship spotted the wreck and signalled for the lifeboats.

The steam lifeboat left Harwich about 9 a.m., seven hours after the ketch had struck, with the pulling-and-sailing lifeboat in tow. When, nearly two hours later, the lifeboatmen saw the masts of the *DAYS* above the grey water the steam lifeboat swung round so that the men in the sailing lifeboat could attempt to make their grapnels fast in the rigging.

Time and again the grapnels broke away, but at last a line was thrown into the rigging and first one and then the other shipwrecked sailor was hauled through the surf to the lifeboat. Coxswain William Tyrell, of the *DUKE OF NORTHUMBERLAND*, looked at the two rescued men and then at the boy's body still hanging in the rigging. But he must not wait to recover the boy for he was already dead, and his business was with the living. He swung the wheel and set course for Harwich, where the two rescued men were cared for at the Great Eastern Hotel.

Later in the day the steam lifeboat returned to the wreck to recover the body of the boy. One of the crew, John Mills, jumped from the *DUKE OF NORTHUMBERLAND* into the rigging to cut the lashing which held the corpse to the shrouds—then he had to be dragged through the water on the end of a rope just as Skipper Sweeting and Edward Hamilton had been a few hours earlier.

Those were busy days for the Harwich lifeboats.

From *Wreck and Rescue on the Essex Coast*
by Robert Malster, 1968.

HAZARDS OF SALVAGING

ON November 10 (1834) the Colne smack *EAGLE*, with William Easter master, was hove to on the look-out in the Swin off the Crouch. It was about eleven in the morning, blowing a hard gale from the E.N.E., and thick with rain, when they saw a vessel go ashore on the Middle Sand. Letting draw, they found her to be the 600-ton barque *MARQUIS OF HUNTLY* sailing from Leith to London with Government stores. She had a pilot on board, but had no idea of her position. Other smacks were already on the scene, including the *BATCHELOR*.

It was a terrible business getting aboard, and in doing so the *BATCHELOR'S* boat was swamped, the master, Lawrence, being washed out of her and rescued with great difficulty. However, they got under her lee and aboard in the end, and Easter was put in charge. He had the main try-sail and spanker set and got her head to wind; then the jib and fore-topmast-staysail were set to drive her off, but when the fore-tops'l filled the yard carried away. The salvagers then turned attention to lightening the ship and managed to get six heavy cannon and some chests of ammunition overboard, a Herculean task as they had to dump them to wind-ward to save her smashing in her lee bilge on them. All this time the barque was pounding violently, decks awash. Now they let go the starboard bower anchor and awaited the next tide.

The captain wanted to send to Sheerness for a steamer. Easter disagreed, saying they would be afloat or broken up before she could arrive. Two brothers named Cook and a man called Samuel Wisbey manned their boat, however, and attempted to get back to the smack for the purpose. The boat capsized, and the three were drowned under the eyes of their mates.

When the tide came the anchor-chain crushed the iron fairlead and nearly took the stem out, but they got a spring on it. When this parted she bore off the wrong way, and they lost three more boats alongside, and nearly a lad with them, for he was in the water for twenty minutes. Eventually they wore her round, and at half-past six that evening she was afloat in Swin without her false keel. They pumped all night, and next day Easter took her to Gravesend.

From *The Last Stronghold of Sail*
by Hervey Benham, 1948.

CAPTAINS COURAGEOUS

THOUGH it can boast no early circumnavigators of the globe, Essex in its time has produced some truly remarkable seafarers. There was for example Robert Moore, of Harwich, who played the leading part in an action against a Turkish galley and was instrumental in freeing 266 Christian slaves from their servitude. All England in 1579 resounded with his praise.

Another seaman of nation-wide renown was the Harwich shipmaster Thomas Thompson, who rose to be one of the six " principal masters of the Navy"—a position of high responsibility. There was a dash of the pirate in his make-up, however, and the greatest moment of his career came in 1592 when he sailed into Harwich harbour in a vessel owned by Sir John Hawkins—the *Dainty*—with her holds full of Spanish treasure. Skipper and crew paraded the streets with their spoils, and the day, with its auction sales, tavern brawls and singing of sea shanties, was remembered for decades after.

Enumerated among the shipmasters of Harwich in 1582, six years prior to the sailing of the great Armada, were John and Thomas Gray, who acted as the captains of small but highly combative fighting ships. John in fact rose to be master of the *Revenge*, Drake's flagship in 1588, though he had flown the Jolly Roger at an earlier stage of his career. There had actually been a warrant out against him in 1567 for piracy. Thomas Gray was master of the *Ark Royal*, flagship of the fleet in Armada year . . .

The capture of the great Spanish treasure ship *Madre de Dios* is inseparably associated with the name of another Harwich ship-master, Christopher Newport, a man of dominating personality who in 1591-2 sailed to the West Indies in command of an expedition consisting of the *Golden Dragon* and three other vessels. He visited Hispaniola, Cuba, Honduras and Florida, sacked their principal cities and either captured or destroyed a score of Spanish ships.

It was following these exploits on the voyage home that he hailed Sir John Burgh, a friend of Raleigh, and assisted in the attack on the *Madre de Dios*—the " great carrack " as she was called. The action against her began at Flores, in the Azores, on August 3, 1592, and lasted sixteen hours. When, at the end of a stubborn fight, she was boarded the English sailors were astounded by the fabulous riches she carried. Stowed away in her capacious holds was a cargo estimated to be worth £250,000 in terms of Elizabethan currency . . .

The victorious fleet returned to England in safety . . . (and) returning . . . to the *Madre de Dios*, it was Christopher Newport, most famous of the Harwich shipmasters, who took command of her on the homeward voyage. He brought his prize safely into Dartmouth harbour on September 7, 1592, and from the Devon port sailed in Hawkins's ship the *Dainty* for Harwich, bearing with him his own share of the plunder . . .

From *Discovering the Essex Coast*
by Rudolph Robert, 1969.

THE EAST COAST PACKET

FOR just two centuries His Majesty's mails, and many of his subjects from the humblest to the haughtiest, were carried in little sailing packet-boats across that unfriendly hundred miles of the

North Sea that tosses and tumbles between Harwich and Holland . . .

The story of the packet-boats is a colourful tale. If one wants to go back to the beginning it was to Harwich that the first naval dispatch in English history was brought. It was brought in the cog *Thomas* from Edward III, to his son, the Black Prince, left behind at Shotley when his father sailed from Harwich to Sluys, there to win the great sea battle of 1340. Harwich had been a packet port in the days of the Hanse merchants, but the regular Dutch service did not open till the seventeenth century.

The Post Office packets were approximately contemporary with the revenue cruisers; indeed, the two services have much in common. Both carried out arduous duties in cutters, which were just beginning to develop into schooners when the end came. Both fleets were mostly owned by private contractors, and though the later Post Office boats at Harwich were seldom of over 70 tons, and were thus less ambitious than the customs cruisers, their adventures were in some ways yet more stirring, for in addition to smelling their share of powder their captains had to display immense judgement and dash to snatch passages in the dead of winter . . .

Certainly the Harwich packets regarded themselves as a little fleet with their own rights, privileges and traditions. The first Post Office agent, Thomas Langley, who was also Mayor of the town, styled himself " Commander " of the packet service, and during the French wars the boats carried their own " post-boy jack " to safeguard them from the attentions of English men-of-war and privateers.

From *Once Upon a Tide*
by Hervey Benham, 1955.

THOSE LOVELY, LOVELY CURVES

To watch a barge tacking up-river with a spring tide in a smart breeze of a wind is a sight to see. Unless you knew the power of the tide you would think she must inevitably hit a buoy, but no—she is carried on far beyond it until the edge of the mud is almost reached. The steersman turns his iron wheel and the barge's huge staysail becomes limp. But only for a moment. Tremendous booms, like the discharge of guns afar off, sound across the river as the mighty sail flacks head to wind. The topsail, seen edge on, becomes to all appearances thin, like a handkerchief. But not for long. Soon the noise is augmented by the mainsail as it swings to and fro on its gigantic sprit. The mizzen, which is attached to the rudder, also moves over from one side to the other but in sedate fashion, like a foreman watching to see that everything 'forrard' is properly done—as though it had charge of everything and was not to be hustled. The barge swings round catching as she turns a dollop of sparkling water rainbowed in the sun at her bows. The staysail, now all aback and shoving mightily, is let fly. The wind, filling the great brown canvas sails, sets them once again into those lovely, lovely curves as the vessel, heeling a little now, gathers way, and is off on the other tack.

From *Tideways and Byways of Essex and Suffolk*
by Archie White, 1948.

"*A FOINE SET O' MIN*"

"SMUGGLERS," said Father William, "th' Lord love an' keep ye! I knows a might about they. Do ye plenish me fire an' draw th' curtain, an' I'll tell ye 'bout 'em . . .

"When I were a boy, th' river were full on 'em. Come across th' water from 'Olland, what's out that way, I'm told. Come wi' rum, an' gin, an' bacca, an' lace, same 's what wimmen wear in Lunnon. Lord! I weren't on th' marsh wi' me sheepses f'r nothin'. There's many things I seed, bein' very 'eedful . . . It's many a cargo I've seed run up the river; an' when I were a young man, 'twerent 'Cise-men nor Revvy cutters, neither, what could stop they. The boats used to come wi' the toide, an' drop th' stuff wi' floats an' sinkers, an' then out they'd goo agen; an' if chance toimes they met a Reveny cutter, they was jest 'ard-workin' fisher-folk what 'adn't never done no 'arm to nobody. An' then th' little boats 'd put out o' 'ere an' bring th' stuff ashore, an' bury some on it, an' take the rest inland, wery slow like an' careful. Lord! I've knowed th' 'Cise-men to come a-gallopin' down th' road, an' a score o' bar'ls under th' hedge right in sight, if it 'adn't bin so dark, th' fools! . . . Love ye, I'm some sorry they've all went . . . They've broke it up wi' coast-guardses, an' p'licemen what lives on th' river, an' 'spectors, an' sich like. An' th' men what did ut is dead, an' they schools ha' spoilt th' young 'uns. A man don't belong to hisself no more, an' th' business is gone, like them what did ut. Them what should ha' bin runnin' 'bacca an' gin like ther fathers afore 'em, an' bringin' somethin' chance times to a pore ole man what gives ther fathers good adwice, they're jest fishin' f'r dabs, or shooting on t' sea-wall, or down at th' Wheatshiff, drinkin' stuff what ain't 'arf so good, an' costs 'em 'most fower toimes as much. An' I ain't no patience wi' they. An' I don't take n' count o' fish, an' never did, an' they buds is some 'ard to pluck, for me fingers is wery stiff, an' I keeps all on a breakin' o' the skin. But I've me ole corkscrew, an' do ye look at ut starin' at ye fr' th' wall, an' no wark f'r th' pore thing to do these days. There's toimes when I goos out into me garden an' looks out o'er th' river, an' well I sees ut, not bein' loike them what shuts therselves up, an' cain't even stan' in front o' a drop o' good rine. An' th' wind's right, an' th' toide's right, an' I count th' place they calls 'Olland ain't bin shifted. If ther was 'arf th' pluck ther used to be when I wor a lad, they'd be out wi' th' boats, an' ye'd see some o' they big-sail'd luggers a-turnin' in fr' th' main, an' all th' stuff o'erboard down be Cripple's Creek, an' th' lights a-shinin', an' th' horses a-gallopin', an' folk lookin' out o' th' winders, though they dussent never show n' lights. Ah, they was a foine set o' min, an' we shaint see th' likes o' they in these parts agin."

From *A Countryside Chronicle*
by S. L. Bensusan, 1907.

STILL A WORLD OF SAIL

. . . I LEFT the sea . . . and worked ashore, trying to convince myself that no one with any sense ever went to sea, especially in sail. The shore held great possibilities for a man, I argued with myself, opportunities to plan and prospects of rich reward for his labours; whereas the sea held out nothing but the prospect of years of hard work, long hours, sleepless nights and but little in the way of hard cash. And I believe that I would there and then have finished with going to sea and satisfied myself with a bit of yachting had I not been fool enough to take a job within easy access of the Port of London.

More and bigger ships were using the river, and once or twice I spent my spare hours walking the banks of the lower reaches, watching the interminable stream of traffic on the tideway. Great liners stood out like giants among the myriads of tugs and lighters, the bustling colliers from the north, and crowds of small Dutch motor ships, which at that time were collaring our coastal trade with cheap freights. But it was the red-sailed sailing barges that took my fancy as they threaded their way to and fro, looking very stately and dignified amidst that horde of power driven, smoke-grimed, soulless ruffians. For all their slab sides and flat bottoms the barges were real ships in comparison with the noisy mechanical contraptions which were for ever threatening to run them down . . .

I was standing by the lock gates of the Royal Albert Dock one day and a grey steel barge named the *Reminder* was waiting to go out into the river. She lay in the lock with her topsail sheet out, looking rather gawky and awkward among the bunch of craft around her. Then as the lock gates opened there came a rattle of her topsail halliard block, the screech of a brail winch, a fluttering of white canvas as the big staysail went up the topmast stay; and within a matter of moments she was a cloud of sail. All this was done by two men, the skipper and mate, an impossible feat in any other type of vessel. These barges only carry two men except the very big ones who have three on long coastal voyages.

But it was the sight of the *Reminder* going out of the dock that day and sailing away in the sunshine down Gallions Reach towards her own peaceful Essex shore that finally put paid to my ideas of settling down ashore.

Before I quite realised what I was about or had considered the consequences of my actions, I found myself mate of the sailing barge *Audrey*, trimming coal at Beckton Gasworks where we were loading for Southend. And was I sorry? Well, that was a long time ago and I'm not sorry yet. For, although the schooners were nearly all gone, here was a new life, a new world, but it was still a world of sail.

From *Coasting Bargemaster*
by A. W. Roberts, 1949.

" *A WET SHIRT AND AN 'APPY 'EART* "

AUTHORITIES from Marco Polo to Dr. Johnson have shaken their wise heads over the desperate situation of men who go to sea, and my own preference is every time for the friendly, characterful coastal waters over the cold, deep sea and inhospitable wide oceans. Bargemen go to sea, yet keep one foot ashore. They make the best of both worlds, and the variety of their life enriches their calling and their characters.

The joy of the job is that the barge has never carried any crew. A skipper, a mate, and till recently a boy, who was really an apprentice, form a combination to bring out the best in human nature. Each must work; each is a free man. There is no gold lace giving itself airs aft, no grimy complement performing a labourer's function for'ard. No wonder sailormen have developed a philosophy all their own, combining dash and devilry with simplicity, humour, tolerance and patience.

From *Down Tops'l*
by Hervey Benham, 1951.

Section 4

SOME ESSEX CHARACTERS

THE SALT OF THE EARTH

THIS Essex coast breeds a strange, fierce love of itself. It is a country for men who love solitude and the silence of the sea. Its own men, the fishermen and fowlers, the winklers and shepherds, the bargemen and marsh " lookers," with here and there still an ancient with gold ear-rings in his ears and still, in quiet creek-head villages, " wise women," who will charm your warts away and cure your cows, these people are a race apart. They are the authentic salt of the earth, as salty in mind, as bracing in speech as the sea-verges which nursed them. They are supreme individualists, fierce in independence, polite with nature's own courtesy and witty with that spontaneous wit which puts the townsman's thought-out, reiterated jokes to shame. For though you will often enough hear apt aphorisms, shrewd comments, sly digs and gusty jokes, they are always born of the moment and seldom repeated. There is no dreary attempt to raise a laugh with stale cleverness.

Their names alone are guarantee of their lineage, of pedigrees longer and blood more ancient than that of half the people who add strange decoration to our peerage.

From *The Coast of Enchanted Wings*
by J. Wentworth Day, 1946.

TYBURN DICK

RICHARD Savage, the second but only surviving son and heir of Thomas, 3rd Earl Rivers, . . . was born about 1660, and on the death of his father, September 14th, 1694, succeeded to the title and to the estates in Cheshire and Essex . . .

Sometimes known as " Tyburn Dick," Richard Savage was M.P. for Wigan in 1681 . . . He was the first nobleman and indeed one of the first persons to desert James II on the landing of the Prince of Orange, in whose reign and that of Queen Anne he proved himself to be an eminent soldier and statesman. He attended King William in all his campaigns . . .

In the reign of Queen Anne he was sent in 1706 with an expedition fitted out to make a descent on France . . .

In 1711 he was appointed Envoy Extraordinary to Hanover, to assure the Elector that Queen Anne would take special care to leave the succession of the crown secured to his family. In January, 1712, he was made Master-General of the Ordnance, and, in June of the same year, General and Commander-in-Chief of the Queen's land forces in Great Britain.

The Earl married Penelope, daughter of John Downes, by whom he had one daughter, Elizabeth . . . He had by Elizabeth Culleton an illegitimate daughter, Bessy; and the unfortunate Richard Savage, the poet, claimed, and was generally believed, to have been his natural son by the Countess of Macclesfield.

Macky in his *Characters* thus speaks of him when turned 40: " He was one of the greatest rakes in England in his younger days . . . " To which Dean Swift adds (in 1712) " An arrant knave in common dealings and very prostitute . . . He has left a legacy to about twenty paltry old whores by name, and not a farthing to any friend, dependant or relation."

Adapted from *The Lieutenants and Keepers of the Rolls of the County of Essex*
by Col. Sir Richard Colvin, K.C.B., C.B., T.D., B.A., 1934.

GAMMER MIGGS

Mr. Gage, who lately made some money in the African market and has bought a loud car, came to a halt before the cottage door for the first time. He, and his wife who matches the car admirably, took a large tea, as became their wealth, and sent Gammer Miggs toddling down the path with provender for the chauffeur.

" Lizzie," said Mr. Gage, " this is one of those old country cottages you hear of. That desk, " he indicated the bureau, " is better than the one old Diamond asked seventy-five for. I'll have a try for it."

Gammer Miggs returned.

" You've some pretty old pieces here, ma'am," said Mr. Gage.

" Belonged to me pore gran'mother," replied Gammer Miggs. " I reckon they're good, but I've none to leave 'em to, more's th' pity."

" I'd give you a ten-poun' note for that old desk," said Mr. Gage, and Gammer Miggs laughed merrily.

" I was offered forty-five, that ain't a week ago," she replied, " by a gent what called hisself a dealer, but I sez ' no.' I want fifty if I sell me Gran'mother's piece what she was that fond of. He should say he couldn't gimme no more, bein' he'd have to cart it to Lunnon."

" Fifty's a lot of money," said Mr. Gage.

" That's a reg'lar owd piece, mind ye," shrilled Gammer Miggs. " I ain't purtendin' that's new 'cause it ain't. I 'ouldn't sell it to ye f'r new. That's seen its best days, like me, more's th' pity. I've often said I'd like to get riddy o' them chairs too, but parson sez they're wuth twenty pou's a piece to sell agen. ' Mrs. Miggs,' he sez, bein' that's me name, ' you don't wanter sell such things,' he sez. ' Telly e'r why. Do, folks round here'd be reg'lar vexed, there ain't a many housen wi' sech showpieces.' That's what he called 'em. A man wanter be reg'lar rich to buy sech." She dusted one tenderly.

Twenty-four hours later Mr. Gage accompanied a motor-van to Gallows Green, paid over a three figure sum in Treasury Notes and helped to pack chairs, bureau, gate-legged table and a couch. By nightfall they were safely disposed in an expensive flat on the edge of Belgravia. Gammer Miggs shed a few tears, seemingly of sorrow.

" I'll have to buy a few owd sticks, steddy they," she cried. " I am wholly thankful me pore Gran'mother's safe in Heaven. Didn't, she'd look wunnerful ole-fashioned at me, I be bound."

But when Mr. Gage had gone Gammer Miggs dried her tears, bought largely of shrimps from the carrier's cart and hobbled to the post office with a letter to Messrs. Dearlove and Havingham, the celebrated manufacturers of Jacobean furniture near the Hop Exchange.

"Lummy," said Mr. Dearlove, to his friend and partner on the following morning (he speaks like that), "Granny Miggs has put it across 'em again."

"Three times in fifteen months, Bob," replied Mr. Havingham joyfully; "it's the white hair and wrinkles does it. You'd better pick her out some more. It ought to be looking as though it belonged, by Easter."

Twenty-four hours later another collection of furniture as old but no older than that purchased by Mr. Gage was delivered at the cottage on Gallows Green.

From *Dear Countrymen*
by S. L. Bensusan.

OWD BILL

Owd Bill! Why everybody knaow owd Bill;
He's olluz schemin', olluz at some gaime,
Olluz a actin', tha's what he is; still
You can't help likin' of him all the saime.

A rum un? I sh'd rather think he were!
T'd taike yer all yer time to tackle he.
An' langwidge? Lor, j'yer ever hear him swear?
A mark on swearin'? Ah, sir, that he be.

You might as lief be talkin' to a paost
As try to maike owd Bill amen' his ways;
He knaow his way about as well as maost—
I ne'er see sich a chap in my born days.

You on'y got to say 'I bet yer don't',
An' Bill'll do it, don' care what it be.
He'll best yer, too, I'm bothered if he 'ont;
There's no man livin' dussent tackle he.

Las' Michaelmas us fellers got him on
Down at the Anchor, Sunday dinner time.
There was a good few on us—me, an' John,
An' Steve, an' Tom, an' Sandy Wha's-his-naime.

I don't ezackly knaow how that began.
Several come in—along the rest was Mike.
'Owd Bill,' he say, 'I'll lay a tanner, man,
As you carn't eat a pound o' raw bif staike.'

Owd Bill, o' course, je took him like a shot,
Blest if he didn't do it, too, an' so!
A pound o' raw bif staike! He et the lot,
An' taters, an' a dish of broccolo.

He never goo to Charch, a Sunday, Bill,
Excep' he keep a larkin' all the time.
A reglar bad un, tha's what he is; still
You carn't help likin' of him all the saime.

Why, up at Mis'ley—that there poachin' fray,
I'll lay yer tuppence Bill was in the spree,
But he can olluz faike the thing some way
Afore the Magistrates, so he git free.

He done it, right enough. You woon believe
The times an' times I sin him arter hares.
I could a towd 'em thay was up his sleeve—
Nao, not the rabbits, sir, nao, nao, the snares.

Oo, he's the artfullest you ever knaowed;
He never taike no hart, not anywhere.
There's nao mistake, Bill, he's as owd as owd,
He'd best the very Owd-un, I declare.

Nowhere there ent a bad un t'ekal he—
I knaow there ent a bigger liar livin'

Yet when the day of Judgmen' come you'll see,
He'll faike it somehow so he git to Hiven.

From *Essex Ballads*
by Charles Edwin Benham, 1895.

THE WIDOW MOOR

THE Widow Moor was no ordinary figure of a woman; her aspect was sufficiently uncanny to strike terror into the hearts of most ordinary mortals. Short and extremely stout, with a pronounced outcrop of swarthy hair on her chin and upper lip, she gave the impression of a man in woman's clothing and not at all a prepossessing kind of man either. In addition she carried in her hand a crooked stick of immense length which served to intensify the amazing breadth and squatness of her figure.

" Ho! Muster Knowall," she said, in a deep manlike voice, and the " Ho! " conveyed a very definite challenge mingled with a certain somewhat ogreish enjoyment. " And what be you doin' here? "

Mr. Peacock hesitated, gathering his somewhat flustered wits together in an attempt to suggest some plausible explanation of his desire to seek counsel of the Widow Moor.

" I—I was jus' a thinkin'," he mumbled, " as ye might be wantin' a looker being ye'v got over plentiful o' rabbits ter year—a spoilin' everything th' are . . . "

The widow spat with the sudden, effortless and surprising abruptness of a toad and regarded him reflectively. There was something peculiarly toadlike about her.

" Thank ye, Muster Knowall," she said at length. " I got a looker and that don't cost me nuthen neether—stan's close up agin ye now that do," she added cryptically.

Mr. Peacock glanced nervously around, but could see nobody.

The widow regarded him with a twinkle in her eyes.

" Goo ter th' stile agin ye. Ye'll see 'un a-stannen there, " she said. " Goo ye and have a look," and she pointed to the stile fronting her across the lane.

Sam walked to the stile and glanced cautiously over. A few yards down the field and hidden from the immediate view of the lane by the thickness of the hedge stood the figure of the mawkin . . .

" . . . There ain't none stan's there 's I kin see save th' owd mawkin," he said, " and that 'ont ketch nothen'," he added.

The widow's eyes rested on him with a glint denoting a superior and somewhat contemptuous knowledge.

" That'll ketch jus' what tha's bid," she said impressively, " whether tha's men or rabbits that'll ketch 'em ef tha's bid. That's set ther' a puppus Muster Knowall. Set ther' a puppus that is."

Sam stared at her open mouthed . . .

A slight wind set the pivoted head of the figure nodding . . . and Mr. Peacock became suddenly aware of an unpleasing chill in the surrounding air and began to shuffle his feet.

" Count I'll be a gittin' back ter mine," he said, " don't that'll be gittin' dark afore long. Evenin' ter yer missus," and he turned and began to make his way down the folly, acutely conscious as he moved off of the impact of four eyes derisive and watchful fixed on his retreating back.

He did not stop to gather up his snares for the widow was watching him, and there would be time enough to do so at day-break on the following morning when the coast would be clear . . .

From *The Magic Mawkin and other Essex Tales*
by H. Cranmer-Byng.

OLD DUMMY

In 1863 . . . a very old man whose tongue had been cut out, nobody knew when or why or where, and who was also deaf, had come from Braintree to Sible Hedingham about eight years earlier. He lived in a mud hut, and the villagers nicknamed him " Dummy." They knew that he was a foreigner, and assumed him to be a Frenchman—partly, perhaps, because he kissed the hand of any person who did him a kindness. He walked about wearing two or three hats and two or three coats, and was usually accompanied by two or three little dogs. In order to live he told fortunes, though it is not easy to imagine how he did so . . .

Now, " Dummy " found himself one evening in the small village of Ridgewell, and here he knocked at the door of Mrs. Emma Smith's cottage and asked by signs whether she would put him up for the night. She said that she would not, and " Dummy " trudged away, angrily. Soon afterwards Emma Smith went sick. She assumed at once that " Dummy " had bewitched her, and she was determined that he should spend a night in her cottage so that his spell might be lifted. At last she found him in the *Swan*, a public-house which stood in the middle of Sible Hedingham, close to a brook: but " Dummy " suspected dirty work and refused to oblige her. Their quarrel brought half the village to the *Swan*, and so fierce was the local feeling against the old man that he was rather severely manhandled. The ring-leader of the half-drunken crowd was a young carpenter named Samuel Stammers. At closing time Stammers and his allies followed old " Dummy " out of the inn . . .

Mrs. Smith, shrieking at " Dummy," tearing off his coat and striking him with a stick, then dragged him towards the brook, pushed him into it, and as he was struggling out on the farther bank, hurried over a small bridge where, assisted by Stammers, she threw " Dummy " back into the water. Once again he scrambled out, but this time Mrs. Smith's husband came up to reinforce the carpenter, and picking up " Dummy " by the legs and the armpits, the two men cast him into the deepest part of the water. The crowd then became slightly apprehensive for themselves lest " Dummy " should actually drown, and for this reason he was permitted in the end to creep away to his hut, and here—soaked and bruised—he lay down at last. About a month later he died in the workhouse.

Smith and Stammers . . . had thrown " Dummy " into the water, of course, by reason of the old notion that a witch or a wizard will float and cannot be drowned. What strange and dreadful story could the destitute and aged Frenchman have told concerning his early life? He is said to have been " eighty or perhaps eighty-six " when he died. He may, therefore, have lost his tongue in the Revolution.

From *Highways and Byways in Essex*
by Clifford Bax, 1939.

Chelmsford as it was in the days when cattle were driven down the centre of the High Street.

Even in the days when passengers arrived by horse-drawn transport the railway station at Chelmsford presented a busy scene.

Trams and horseless carriages began to supersede the horse in the early years of thi
century, as this photograph of Colchester High Street shows.

Hot and cold sea water was available for bathers at the pier, Clacton-on-Sea, in the ear
years of the century.

There were more pedestrians than traffic in the old High Street at Grays.

Judging by the worn steps the old town pump at Southminster was very much used.

No doubt Gigney's Bonus Stores of Wickford were very proud of their brand-new For
with its modern acetylene lamps.

There are still people who remember the hailstones that fell during the storm of May 2
1913. The egg in the centre gives an idea of the size of the hail.

Some of the damage that was caused by the earthquake in Essex in 1884. This photograph shows the Bell at Old Heath.

Rayleigh in the days when there was a cattle market in the main street but very little traffic.

A view from the Palace hotel at Southend-on-Sea dated 1911.

The beach at Southend-on-Sea long before the present development took place.

Westcliff Parade at Southend-on-Sea presented a busy scene on summer days before the Kaiser's war.

There were many enterprising costumes and much hilarity at the Woodford meet. This photograph of a club tableau, " Bluebell's dream," was taken in 1911.

The beach at Walton-on-the-Naze attracted many holidaymakers in days gone by. The clothing seems quite suitable for cold winds off the North Sea, then called the German Se

Another view of Walton-on-the-Naze.

FATHER WILLIAM

"It's a gret ole pity that they ever 'ad a schoolmaster in Maychester," Father William remarked . . . "If they'd ha' gie'd me 'is 'ouse and 'is money, I'd ha' done better be 'em, an' that's th' truth. They might ha' kep' th' gels, f'r I can't abide 'em, but they might ha' sent th' lads to me."

"But what about their lessons?" I replied.

"I don't take no count o' they," said Father William emphatically, "an' never didn't, f'r they ain't done 'em no good be no means. If a boy's smart 'e'll pick up 'is letters . . . I didn't 'ave no larnin', but I'm th' wery oldest man in th' parish an' wery respected . . ."

He paused awhile; it has become an ever-increasing effort of late years to lay down the law.

". . . I could ha' started afore ye were born. I'd ha' took th' lads an' taught 'em to goo strite. I'd ha' taught 'em to 'andle a spide proper, an' to grow wegebles an' tend sheepses an' grow fruit an' keep their vermin down. There 'ouldn't ha' bin a gret ole rat in all Maychester. An' I'd ha' mide 'em respectful; didn't, I'd ha' welted 'em. An' I'd ha' took th' wery best an' made p'licemen on 'em, else shepherds, an' I'd ha' separated up t'others f'r t'other jobs. It all comes o' shepherdin'. Ye learn what every shep is good for, whether f'r lambin' or fattin' or sendin' to th' show, or sellin' to them what don't know nothin'. An' a boy's wery like a shep, 'cept that 'e costs more to keep an' ain't as waluable, an' nobody can't deny ut."

There was a definite challenge in his tone . . .

"Time I were a boy an' one o' me mates got a job, 'e kep' it until 'e died or was tore out. Once settled, allus settled, that's 'ow it were those days. 'E went strite or 'e went sly; most o' 'em went sly, but 'e did 'is wark an' kep' 'is plice till 'e was broke at ut, an' they took 'im 'ome to th' workus at Market Waldron. Then comes th' schoolmaster, drat 'im, an' th' little ole m'chines what does th' work o' three, an' men went off like rotten sheepses. Th' boys fair ached to goo up to Lunnon, or to goo out furrin in shipses, they grow'd wunnerful oncontented, ye couldn't do nothin' with 'em. An' if so be their master welted 'em, blime me if they didn't summons 'e, an' th' magistrites at Market Waldron told 'im 'e were agin th' law, what 'e never oughter. An' th' lads took to poachin' quite careless an' settin' in th' Wheatsheaf along o' their wery fathers, an' runnin' after th' gels shimeful, th' 'ussies. Why, I've know'd lads what's fathers 'ad bin in one plice all their lives in an' out o' three or four or more time they was five-and-twenty. They'd goo if they didn't like th' looker, or if they thought th' next farmer brewed better beer; I've seed those things along o' me own eyes, an' it's all along o' th' schoolmaster. 'E must ha taught 'em, f'r they didn't know nowt of ut until 'e come. Nobody 'adn't know'd boys that restless an' imperent in th' old times, an' so I'm agin th' schoolmaster, an' I'd tell 'im so wunnerful sharp."

He paused . . . and . . . went on with even greater conviction than before.

" . . . I ses to meself, it's all along o' schools an' readin' an' writin' an' sich.

" . . . if they'd let me look arter th' lads stead o' th' schoolmaster, I'd mike men on 'em 'stead o' fools an' rogues. But there ain't no time. I'm in me ninety, an' Boy Bill's 'most all I can manage. Time's agin' me."

And with these words Father William's head sunk until his white beard and grey cape met, and in a minute a moderate but regular grunt proclaimed full repose.

From *A Marshland Omnibus*
by S. L. Bensusan, 1954.

THE STRONG MAN OF STANSTEAD

JOSLIN was reckoned the strongest man in Stanstead, and, before this poaching job, no one dared give him back an angry word. He stood six feet high, and was broad in proportion; I've seen him take an ass by the mane and tail and lift him about as easily as if it were a little dog.

One day he was going along the road to Stortford, mounted on his own donkey, which was a good-sized animal, when he came to the turnpike gate just past Zion House. He asked the pikeman how much would be charged for his donkey to walk through.

" Two pence," was the reply. " And how much do you charge for carrying a parcel through the gate?" " Nothing," says the pike-man. " Whoa, ass, whoa," cries Joslin, and, quietly dismounting, he deliberately slips his head under the animal's belly, and seizing his fore legs with his hands, lifts him off the ground and carries him through the gate, setting him down on the other side. " Gee up, Noddy," says he, getting on the donkey's back, and on he goes.

From *The Autobiography of an English Game-keeper, John Wilkins*, edited by A. H. Byng and S. M. Stephens, 1892.

OLD SYD

OLD Syd is *very* ' Essex,' and often I have to be told, by way of translation, that a ' ship ' is a sheep, ' brown-typhus ' bronchitis, and a ' ship-dawg ' a sheepdog; and I love the soft, slow burr with its wonderful old-time expressive language.

" Memories being what I got lots on," he began, " I often set here a-using on 'em up, and some queer things come to mind.

" I 'member one of my very first jobs was to goo and tell the bees my grandfather have died. P'raps you never heard o' that, but it were handed down that all them what have bees must do this—one of the family, or someun near to 'em, *must* goo and tell the bees who it is have died so they'll settle down and not leave the hives. They do say this really come from Suffolk in the first place, but if it do then Essex have stuck to it ever since.

" Some time back I have a man come here to ask what I could tell about a right o' way that run through a certain field round Bradwell way and have some people a-fighting about it.

" It happen that I have knowed that path since I were a boy, and mind my father telling me how sich were first made. P'raps a man goo and die in a place where there's no roads, and naturally they carry him down to the churchyard the shortest way, crorst the countery as the crow floy, and sich carrying of a corpse make the path a ' right-a-way ' autometical, and everyone accept it.

" There were one sich as run right atween two hobbly old houses which were left empty, and reckoned to be haunted, the path being cursed. The mystery attracts us boys and we keep daring one another to look inside, but wuz all too scairt because of the strange noises gooing on.

"One owner had been a 'snob,' and my father say it were his ghost trying to get boots on his sore feet when he goo a-haunting. Then he laugh and say it must be pritty hard to do it because a ghost don't have nawthin to pit inside the boots, which account for the scuffling.

" Well, one evening I get my grit and gristle up and break in, and blow me if I weren't half smothered in the warm, furry bodies, all over me. I wuz afeered they'd be rats, but they wuz rabbuts, a colony of 'em *upstairs*, too.

" I bring two rabbuts home, and get a clip on the yurr for gooing there, and a pat on the back for not being too duckhearted to goo. The food was welcome as there wuz eleven of us in the family . . . "

From *Essex Countryside*,
by Alfred A. Payne, 1967.

POOR OLD PHILLIPS

OLD Phillips had a curious and terrible dream one night, and it made such an impression on him that he related it to his mates in the harvest field next day . . . They were at work in the field, and at noon they sat down to dinner, when Phillips related his dream. He said he dreamed that he was minding a team of horses and a waggon in the field, carting the harvest; he described the field and a few of his companions then around him, all of which he saw in a dream. He went on to say that he took hold of one of the horses by the leading rein, was knocked down and killed.

No one paid much attention to his story at the time, but about half-an-hour afterwards, on their getting up from their meal to resume work, Phillips went up to one of the horses attached to a waggon, to put his bridle on, or do something with the bridle. Just at this moment a fly bit the horse, causing him to swing his head round to his shoulder, in order to knock off the fly, when the bridle ring of the bit caught in the hook of the shaft, so as to prevent the horse bringing his head back into place again. This of course very much frightened the animal, which turned restive and plunged about, at length breaking away from Phillips, and galloping wildly off. Phillips was knocked down and the waggon passed over him, crushing his head out quite flat; the wheels carried away his brains and portions of his skull for a long distance, and they had great difficulty in gathering up the remains of his crushed head. It was fearfully mutilated, and they were obliged to collect dirt, stubble, brains and bones, all together, and bury them.

Such was the end of Phillips; he died with an oath on his lips, " damning " the horse to " stand still " when it became restive, so he was suddenly destroyed without remedy . . .

From *The Autobiography of an English Gamekeeper, John Wilkins,*
edited by A. H. Byng
and S. M. Stephens, 1892.

THE FIGHTING PARSON

HENRY BATE, afterwards the Rev. Sir H. Bate-Dudley, Baronet, was born in the little desolate fen parish of North Farnbridge (A.D. 1745), where his father was then rector. Bate seems to have entered at Queen's College, Oxford, but it appears open to question whether he ever took his degree. He subsequently took holy orders, and in due course succeeded his father at North Farnbridge. But the retirement of a country rectory suited him but little, and the greater portion of his time seems to have been passed in London. In the year 1773 the " Fighting Parson," as he was already nicknamed, became notorious owing to his participation in a disturbance at Vauxhall . . . Bate became one of the earliest editors of *The Morning Post*, then, as now, a Tory Journal, and in this capacity was celebrated for his contributions to its columns. Quarrelling with the proprietors of the *Post*, however, in 1780, Bate started in the month of November the Liberal *Morning Herald*, and in the same year two other newspapers, one printed in French, styled *Courrier de l'Europe*, the other *The English Chronicle*. The next year Bate became acquainted with the interior of the King's Bench Prison, being committed for twelve months in consequence of a libel on the Duke of Richmond which had appeared in his paper. It was now that he bought the advowson of Bradwell for the sum of £1,500. In the year 1784 he assumed the name of Dudley. The absentee rector of Bradwell dying in 1797, Bate-Dudley presented himself to the living; as a fact, he had acted as curate there for five years previously, during which time he had spent some £28,000 on rebuilding the church, erecting a house, and reclaiming land. Unfortunately for him, however, the Bishop of London was able to raise objections on the score of "simony," during the settlement of which the presentation of the living lapsed to the Crown. Bate-Dudley was thus robbed of the cash expended and the fruits thereof, for the Crown presented the Chaplain-General of the Army to the living. A similar course had been taken in 1640, when the Crown presented Nicholas More to the rectory. It was certainly a very hard case, and public feeling was much in favour of Bate-Dudley. Some amends seem to have been made him by the gift of church preferment in Ireland, and in the year 1813 he was created a baronet. Sir Henry died childless in 1824. His portrait and that of Lady Dudley, by Gainsborough, until a few years ago used to hang in the drawing-room of Bradwell Lodge, now the rectory. It is not often that a man can be found at once parson, duellist, journalist, dramatist and wit, church builder and land reclaimer, courtier, political turncoat, and finally a baronet!

From *Essex: Highways, Byways, and Waterways*
by C. R. B. Barrett, 1892.

Section 5

HEARTH AND HOME

LET NO MAN PUT ASUNDER

MARRIAGE resembles a pair of shears, so joined that they cannot be separated; often moving in opposite directions, yet always punishing anyone who comes between them.

From *Wit and Wisdom*
by Sydney Smith, 1860.

MOST HAPPY HUSBAND

IF thy fancy and judgment have agreed in the choice of a fit wife, be not too fond, lest she surfeit, nor too peevish, lest she languish. Love so, that thou mayst be fear'd: rule so, that thou mayst be honour'd. Be not too diffident, lest thou teach her to deceive thee, nor too suspicious, lest thou teach her to abuse thee. If thou see a fault, let thy love hide it; if she continue it, let thy wisdom reprove it: reprove her not openly, lest she grow bold. Rebuke her not tauntingly, lest she grow spiteful. Proclaim not her beauty, lest she grow proud; boast not her wisdom, lest thou should be thought foolish. Shew her not thy imperfections, lest she disdain thee. Pry not into her dairy, lest she despise thee. Prophane not her ears with loose communication, lest thou defile the sanctuary of her modesty. An understanding husband makes a discreet wife, and she, a happy husband.

From *Enchiridion*
by Francis Quarles (1592-1644).

PROUD PEDIGREE

THE days when men encased themselves in armour and wore surcoats bearing their emblems have long since passed. But the passing of the painted shield and the crested helmet did not mark the extinction of heraldry. On the contrary, it was adapted to many types of decoration which evoke a sense of tradition and chivalry. Whether it exhibits itself in a Grant of Arms, an illuminated pedigree, an estate map, a seal, a piece of plate or embroidery, a funeral hatchment or a bookplate, there is something personal about it, something peculiar to one family or body of people, and therein lies its attraction.

From *Heraldry in Essex*
published by the Essex County Council, 1953.

IN SEARCH OF A COUNTRY RETREAT

MANY years ago, a gentleman who had amassed considerable property in commercial pursuits resolved to retire, purchase an estate, and enjoy for the rest of his life his " otium cum dignitate " in the country. Hearing of some property to be sold in the neighbourhood of Jarvis Hall (Benfleet), and not relying upon his own judgment, which could hardly distinguish light stony land from clay, he brought with him to Southend an estate agent to give sound advice in the matter. Taking a post chaise, they travelled through the fertile parish of Prittlewell, admiring the country and the woods (Wakering wood was then in existence, opposite Lapwater Hall), and so on towards Hadleigh, where the agent began to shrug his shoulders. Hadleigh common, then covered with furze and in a state of nature, abounding with numerous flocks of geese, and studded with tents of wanderers, appeared to Moneybags a scene of rural felicity, and although the turnpikes were voted nuisances, yet the winding road beyond Hadleigh House was thought charming; but when the view near Jarvis Hall, by the road leading to Thundersley, was arrived at, our friend's extacies could no longer be controlled, and his admiration was unbounded. Thoughts of ague were dismissed as chimerical, and every object seemed to gratify. Turning to his agent, he exclaimed with rapture, " This is the place, it is delightful, and I should say healthy; I could live and die here." Trusty, who had been musing, now chimed in, and exclaimed, " No chance of dying, for I'll engage many more run away than die; very healthy, very splendid, beautiful, quite entrancing, but if you ask me for advice where to lay your money out, it certainly is not here, upon a soil that never ought to have been grubbed."

Upon this, his ardour cooled, the horses heads were turned eastward, and all thoughts of purchase abandoned, after taking a last, long and lingering look at the delightful landscape.

From *The History of the Rochford Hundred*
by Philip Benton (1867-86).

A COTTAGE IN THE COUNTRY

THE simple life, the little cottage in the country, was letting us down good and proper . . .

This cottage is full of strange draughts that delight not, and hurt. Sometimes a thousand twangling currents will eddy about my ears, but when it comes to putting on fur gloves to do the daily dozen in the cold bedroom up under the eaves something will have to be done. Mind you, it's a splendid idea when one remembers how one of our babies once, waving her little fists in the pram, got frostbite, having cunningly chewed off her woolly gloves. We don't want to have to resort to the lanoline that cured her.

Another thing, even without gloves one's fingers have to be doubled up lest in one of the more hearty swing-ups the roof gets lifted off . . .

The draughts are strange and intriguing, following no known law. For what selfish reason does one blow out of an empty socket in a beam where once a cross-beam had lain?

And under the stairs which lead straight up into a bedroom there is a little cupboard from which, when you open it, a howling gale rushes out. Funny little cupboard! It is only eighteen inches high, and when its spring hinges snap it to you would never know it was there.

Did some very small man with a large, henpecking wife use it in days gone by as a means of escape, possibly a secret exit to a pub? . . .

On second thoughts the unwanted air may be coming through those knotholes outside. We have plugged up a couple with beer-bottle stoppers. When we have some more beer we might do the lot, then passers-by will think they are bullet marks like those from the civil war in the famous house at Colchester. Sunday traffic jams will be caused as motorists stop to look and we will put up a notice, "Teas served," and make some useful money to pay for the services of some professional draught-stopper ...

Among the strange junk we brought with us by mistake is a South Polar hat worn by a member of the family when out in those regions. Year by year its fur flaps have grown steadily more moth-eaten. We haven't had the heart to throw it away . . . That hat is going to be very useful now.

The draughts may rush down the staircase from tightly closed windows above to chill us at breakfast; they may turn round and rush up again to catch us at the daily dozen; if we are still upstairs they may, if bottled up in one direction, pour through some other little crack with doubly concentrated malice; but what do we care?

In our South Polar hat and our fur gloves we will swing up and down and sideways, defying them to the last...

From *Essex Countryside*
by Bellvine, 1960.

FARMHOUSE MEMORY

In the hot August afternoons, while the cyclists whirred by along the dusty road, we would get over the stile into the fields, and rest on the shady green banks overhanging the river, where the boughs drooped low over the water, and dappled its surface with shadow. Much of the soil beneath the banks had been washed away, exposing the roots of the trees. Now and then a roach would slide out from the weeds and lie luxuriously in the sunlit water where it flowed, pellucid over the gravel. He would perhaps allow your hand to come within a few inches of him, then suddenly dart several yards up stream like a flash of quicksilver.

Not until the cool of the evening when the lights began to gleam across the darkening chase from the windows of the old house, and the dog barked his welcome at the sound of our footsteps, would we return to what we learned to regard as " home." As we fell asleep at night in an exquisitely fresh white room, we would hear the cry of the owl in the great barn, and be wakened in the morning by the plaintive cooing of wood-pigeons in the elms beyond the moat. Such are the peaceful signs that mark the passage of the hours in an Essex farmhouse of the olden time.

From *Romantic Essex*
by Reginald A. Beckett, 1901.

TO STEW CARPS

TAKE your carps and kill them under the gills or tails with a pen-knife and as they bleed you must keep the blood stirring with a little white wine that it clots not together. Then take your carps and scour them with some salt. Then open them and scour them well and put them in your stew-pan or dish and cover them with claret and put in a bunch of sweet herbs, 2 or 3 whole onions and some salt, whole pepper and some large mace and half a nutmeg sliced. Cover them close and let them stew; and when they are about half stewed turn them and then put in the blood, stir it in the liquor they were stewed in and put it in a basin and set it over a chafing-dish of coals with 6 yolks of eggs well beaten and a shallot or two and 2 or 3 anchovies. Let them be dissolved in your sauce; then set it over the fire with the eggs stirring it all the while for fear lest it should curdle them; pour it to your carps and send it in.

Mrs. Elizabeth Slany's Book of Receipts, 1715.

From *English History from Essex Sources*
by A. C. Edwards, 1952.

PORK PLUGGA—AN ESSEX SPECIALITY

Water;
4oz. suet;
8oz. plain flour;

Chopped sage and onion;
Pepper and salt;
Diced streaky pork.

MAKE a suet crust from the suet, flour and water and roll out. Spread with layers of diced pork, onion, and sage, and season. Wet the edges of the crust, then roll up. Wrap the roll in grease-proof paper brushed over with melted fat, twisting the ends of the paper like a sausage, and put the roll in a pudding cloth. Boil in boiling water for 1½ hours or steam for 2-2½ hours. Make a gravy from the pork trimmings and serve pork plugga hot with gravy.

From *Country Dishes*
compiled by Suzanne Beedell, 1962.

HERMIT CRABS . . . BEWARE !

PEOPLE who build should bear in mind how great is their responsibility, for even one . . . eyesore in bricks and mortar . . . visible for miles around, spoils the landscape to a greater or less extent. It asserts itself and attracts the eye whether it will or no; there is no escape from it. I write feelingly in the matter, for I know more than one pretty peep of country whose sylvan loveliness, so charming and restful to the town-tired eye, has to me been for ever destroyed by the unsightly structures raised therein; freaks in bricks and mortar these, caprices in building to laugh at, were it not a matter to grieve about, this ruthless spoiling of scenery. How sadly these prosaic structures contrast with the poems in buildings that our ancestors loved to raise, in a benighted age, when men had their houses fashioned to suit their individual tastes, not as now run up by contract in whole streets, rows and terraces, as like to one another as peas in a pod, and as undesirable to live in as to look upon, the man of to-day having to fit into his dwelling like a hermit crab as best he may. An old-time home . . . is as delightful to gaze upon as any painted picture, and more so than a great many.

A man with no taste may furnish the interior of his house so that it is unutterably vulgar and eye-irritating to the cultivated mind, but this the public do not see and it only affects the owner and his friends; but the exterior of a house more or less concerns everybody, for this becomes a part of the landscape, and either adds to or takes from its beauty. In a thickly populated country like England, whose scenery is so closely associated with the homes of the people, it is terrible to think how much it is in the power of unsympathetic man to rob it of its traditional loveliness.

From *A Tour in a Phaeton*
by James John Hissey, 1889.

Section 6

SCHOOL DAYS

LEARN AND INWARDLY DIGEST . . .

Rules of St. Edward's National Schools, Romford, 1854.

1. Children of the age of 6 years, and upwards, or who are able to read words of one syllable, are admitted by application to the Committee, who meet at the Girl's Class Room, every Monday morning, at 9 o'clock. No child can be admitted at any other time or day. One of the Parents or the Guardian *must* attend with the child to be admitted.

2. The school hours are from 9 to 12 in the morning, and from 2 to 4 in the afternoon. On Sundays the Children meet at half-past 9 in the morning, and at half-past 2 in the afternoon, and every child is required to attend Divine Service in the Parish Church, morning and afternoon.

3. Every Child, not on the Foundation, must pay *TWOPENCE* weekly, on every Monday morning. (In the case of two or more Children in the same family, a deduction from this payment is made.)

4. The Instruction will consist of Scriptural knowledge and Religious Teaching; Reading, Writing, Arithmetic, History, Geography, Grammar, Book-keeping, and Singing. Children will also be instructed in other subjects as far as their ability and the time of their stay at School will allow.

5. Every Boy and Girl, of the age of 13, or upwards, whose conduct has been praiseworthy, will on quitting the School, be presented with a Bible and Prayer Book.

6. Parents are required to send their Children neat and clean, with their hair combed, and properly cut, and their clothes mended.

7. No Child will be allowed to be absent from School without permission from the Master or Mistress. In case of illness, notice should immediately be sent to the School.

8. The Holidays are,—A month at Harvest-time; a fortnight at Christmas; a week at Easter; and two days at Whitsuntide.

9. Annual Examinations will take place, at which Rewards will be given to those Children who are the most deserving in their respective classes.

10. At the admission of any Child, the Parent will be presented with a Copy of these Rules, a strict observance of which must be required.

From *English History from Essex Sources*
by A. F. J. Brown, 1952.

BOYS WILL BE BOYS

THIS church (St. Thomas à Becket, Brentwood) was founded in the Thirteenth Century as a Chapel of Ease to the Mother Church and Parish of South Weald. It is no longer devoted to sacred purposes, but the murmur of a school is heard within its hoary walls . . . For school purposes a boarded floor has been laid above the level of the old pavement, by which the building loses its fair proportions. Great credit is due to the authorities whose care protects this relic from further injury by the boys collected within its walls.

From *Twenty-two of the Churches of Essex*
by George Buckler, 1856.

EDUCATION: Tuppence a Week

Less than 100 years ago Essex children had to pay to go to school, as the rules of Pattiswick Board School show:

" THE School Money is to be brought to the Mistress every Monday morning, and no Child will be admitted without it, the Charge for a single Child is Two-pence per Week; if more than one of a family belong to the School, they will pay one Penny each per week; Children will have to make these Weekly payments whether they come to School or not, unless they are for some particular reason excused."

From *Essex Countryside*,
by A. C. Steynor, 1965.

THESE NEW-FANGLED WAYS

Me, nao, sir, I don't howd 'ith these Board Schools;
Thäy larn the boys too much, my thinkin', now.
An' what I see, there's jest as many fools
As when thäy put the young uns to the plough.

I ent owd-fashn'd, nao, I loike to see
The young uns comin' on. But now-a-däys
They säy an' do sich things git over me,
An' I carnt howd 'ith these new fangled wäys.

I howd 'ith larnin' mind, but let 'em larn
Saime way as I did, not that stuff o' theirs.
Larn 'em the proper wäy to thetch a barn,
Larn 'em the wäy to sao a field o' tares.

Geoggerfy! Now what on arth's the sense
A larnin' of 'em how the moon go roun'?
An' all about Ameriky an' Frence,
An' plaices tother side o' Lunnon town?

My booy he come to me tother night,
'D'yer knaow,' he säy, the Warld an' you an' me
Are tarnin' on our axles—sich a raite
You woon believe? But there, tha's right', says he.

I tarned he on his axles, you be boun',
    I cop he one. That maide me reg'lar riled,
That fairly did. The Warld a tarnin' roun' !
    To hear sich stuff an' nons'nse from a child!

From *Essex Ballads*
by Charles Edwin Benham, 1895.

TEACHER . . . AT TEN BOB A MONTH . . . NEARLY!

I REMEMBER that day as if it were yesterday. A month before I had been accepted by the East Ham education authority as a P.T. That meant that I spent half of each day at the pupil teachers' centre studying for a King's scholarship which would admit me to a teachers' training college at reduced fees. The other half of the day I went to the school to which I was allocated to learn the practical side of the job.

It was an infants' school, and children were then admitted at three years old. The classes were normally of sixty and most of the classrooms were arranged in galleries. I helped the teachers of various classes and prepared a criticism lesson once a week when the headmistress sat in the room and, later, told me all the things I had done wrongly!

I was often posted to the babies' class, where a delightful, capable woman named Miss Christmas was in charge. The little boys as well as the girls wore frocks, and I was surprised to see her turn a new arrival upside down and investigate its underclothes. " It's the only way you can tell if it's a boy or a girl," she explained, smiling at my horrified expression. " Half of them can't talk plainly. If you ask their names they say ' Baby.' "

I learned to teach the hard way, and in time managed to control and interest a class of sixty with no difficulty. I served as a pupil teacher for six years.

That first pay day I was returning in the afternoon to the pupil teachers' centre and met my headmistress.

" The pay clerk came just after you had left this morning," she said, " so I signed for yours and put the packet in my pocket thinking I might meet you."

She handed me the envelope and walked on. I could show you the very spot where that interview took place. I stood still, clutching my pay packet and exulting. For the first time in my life someone thought my work was worth hard cash. I was a wage earner. I had started on my professional career. I was going to earn my living as a teacher.

I walked to the centre in a dream—one walked miles in those days and thought nothing of it. During the afternoon I frequently slipped my hand into my pocket to feel that packet, but I did not open it till I went home to tea.

Then the great moment came. I held my breath as I opened it and the coins fell out. I counted them carefully. The amount was eight shillings and four pence! That was a month's pay, for by my indentures I was employed at £5 a year . . . that was in 1901; I was fifteen and no other cheque or pay packet has ever given me such a thrill.

From *Essex Countryside*
by O. M. Rookwood, 1963.

CORPORAL PUNISHMENT

THERE was a kind of capriciousness about Mr. Stuart's caning that is difficult to explain and almost impossible to understand. This capriciousness—or selectiveness if you like—or perhaps it was a natural modesty, prevented our Headmaster from whacking us on our behinds and we had to endure the much worse punishment of holding out one hand after the other. The dose was always three or six, and if the canee not unnaturally jerked his hand away what had gone before did not count and the execution started all over again.

I have wondered, from time to time, if this hand-caning gave our Headmaster a strange pleasure, but he himself had a much more ingenious and disarming explanation.

Whacking anyone's bottom, Mr. Stuart told us, gave the victim a great feeling of inferiority. It was undignified and, he assured us, it was a matter connected with a very illustrious bottom that had started the 1914 war. Mr. Stuart, it appeared, was not going to start any more wars!

It happened this way. On an occasion during the cruise on the Royal Yacht, while the future King Edward VII was still Prince of Wales, the Kaiser had been one of the guests, and, on one memorable day, the Prince of Wales had spotted the Kaiser leaning over the deck-rail. The Kaiser was dressed in a very tight dress-uniform and the target to the Prince of Wales, who loved rather schoolboyish practical jokes, was irresistible. Creeping up behind his nephew, the Prince of Wales gave him a mighty kick which practically sent him into the ocean. The Prince of Wales roared with delight at this schoolboy fun. The Kaiser did not share his amusement.

'From that day,' said Mr. Stuart, 'war was inevitable.'

Maybe he was right. Anyway, he believed it.

From *Essex Schooldays*
by Simon Dewes, 1960.

THE GIRLS OF ST. MONICA'S

It was with great delight that, after having taught physical education to classes of thirty and forty pupils for most of my teaching career, on my first morning at St. Monica's I faced a class of fourteen girls. They were not sporting the thick woollen gym knickers and long-sleeved blouses which I had somehow always associated with girls' public schools. Instead they wore neat cherry-red shorts and crisp white shirts. Their day uniform of blue-grey pinafore dresses, white blouses and cherry-red ties and cardigans was equally attractive, as were their red straw boaters and hooded winter cloaks.

The girls were polite and friendly, and almost immediately I became a welcome member of their small community.

From *Essex Countryside*
by Valerie M. Carhill, 1970.

"*DEAR SIR . . .*"

ALL teachers know the veteran who complains bitterly of the sad decline in professional standards since his early days in education.

He sometimes produces evidence—beautiful arithmetic books with long and intricate examples neatly and impeccably worked; copper-plate handwriting of superb symmetry; woodwork or needlework of rare finish and patent craftsmanship—and we observers rightly marvel.

In my cynical way I usually rely for a salve on the parents' notes which come every teacher's way. The ones which often begin:

"*Please excuse . . .*"

Jill was unable to attend school on Thursday and Friday owing to school dinner being so rich . . .

Peter was away from school because I have not been well and Dr. would not let me go out, so he had to do errands and keep eye on my baby, he *has not* been pea picking . . .

Coral is free from all spot so is OK for school . . .

Peter was unable to attend school on Tuesday as he was kicked on the head during a game of Football and suffered a severe headache . . .

Stephanie has been away with the flu again and it has left her with catarrh in the ear's. I thought that I would let you know in case she seems a little distant in class. Then you would understand why . . .

Will you please note that Peter will not be able to attend school on Wednesday 1st April . . .

Stephanie is back once again as you will see she is still a little deaf and a bit dull, but I think she will be alright, anyway I hope so . . .

Dudley helped me on Friday last . . .

From *Essex Countryside*
by Leslie Thompson, 1961.

Section 7

ESSEX AT WORK

ROOT OF ALL EVIL

THE necessity of labour may be promoted by the expensive cravings of vice: but then industry is purchased at a rate desperate to the individual, and dangerous to the community.

From *A General View of Agriculture in the County of Essex*
by Charles Vancouver, 1795.

ACTIVE, INTELLIGENT FARMERS

THERE certainly are in this county a number of active, intelligent farmers, who have shewn a laudable spirit of improvement of their lands, and who have spared neither trouble nor expense in making experiments . . .

There is here (as in other counties more or less) one grand obstacle to all improvement; for great as is the industry and judgment of our farmers in the cultivation of their land, still they receive so severe a check to their spirit of improvement, when they see the tythe-owner taking from them a tenth of all their produce, that it frequently puts an end to all enterprise and experiment.

From *A General View of Agriculture in the County of Essex*
by Charles Vancouver, 1795.

HARVEST TIME

THE waggons come and go, the stack grows high,
The chickens search between the horses' hoofs,

And Bob lies stretched out in the summer sun.
The farmer works as second man to Bill,
And Joe is in the hole and pitches thence
To those on top. With nimble feet Bill moves
From place to place and neatly binds the sheaves,
And though the stack is rocking gently, yet
It does not heald at all or look askew.
You get a master view from off the top—
The Farmer shows six churches thereabout:
There's wooded Danbury high to the east,
Great Totham, Waltham, Broomfield, Galleywood
And Baddow, nestling in a scene that would
Have quite rejoiced our English Constable—
White mills, sheer water, slowly-moving stream,
B nt willows, cottage-thatch and trickling lanes
Midst orient lozenges of ripened corn.

From *An Essex Harvest and other Poems*
by H. H. Abbott, 1925.

MOST USEFUL ACQUAINTANCE

CARRIERS take life in a leisurely fashion, like most country people. The times at which they are supposed to start may be taken as approximate. You need not fear being left behind if you do not arrive to the minute, especially if you have told the carrier beforehand that you are coming. If anyone whom the carrier expects does not come at the proper time, the carrier will cheerfully wait half an hour or more. He seems to feel no annoyance at being kept waiting, but much solicitude for the welfare of the loiterer. This sort of thing is only possible in the real country. When at length the horses have been harnessed, and everything arranged in readiness for a start, the carrier, after seeing that all his fellow-travellers are as comfortable as circumstances will permit, mounts to his seat, takes the reins, and with a flourish of his whip drives through the archway into the gabled street. In a very short while the town comes to an end, giving place to fields on either hand and leafy boughs overhead. Every now and then a halt is made at a cottage, or at some stile with a house a field or two behind it, and sundry parcels are exchanged with much leisurely discourse in the broad local dialect. It is really wonderful what complicated messages these carriers manage to remember, and what a variety of commissions they execute in the towns for the isolated country people. This fact was remarked by a clergyman newly come into an Essex parish, who complimented the local carrier upon his powers of mind. " Yes," replied the carrier, in perfect good faith, " if you had my job, you would have to wake up."

Carriers are most useful acquaintances. They know the country and the people—none better—and can often tell you just what you want to know . . . In their company you quickly learn what the people of the district are doing and thinking. They are nearly always cheerful and communicative, and usually themselves full of character.

From *Romantic Essex*
by Reginald A. Beckett, 1901.

LOT No. 121—WHAT AM I BID?

THE auctioneer's voice boomed out: " Now then you butchers and farmers—*this is your day!* There are about twenty lots all, and really good value."

The lots were disposed of quickly and the market seemed pretty good and Harwood felt quite sure that his suggested price would be justified.

" Lot No. 121, three prime fat hogs in excellent condition," continued the auctioneer, " what's that? Someone suggested that I sell them one at a time? I'm not thinking so, of course, if the market really wants such a waste of time it could be done, but remember I'm not going to choose which one you have bought when you come to collect your animal, and I'm not running the figure up three times; if they are to be sold in three lots the bidding the second and third time must start where the first and second left off. So what's it to be? "

" Sell according to catalogue sir," cried two or three voices.

" That's right, thank you gentlemen. Now what shall we say for these three fine hogs? What's that, £7? No, no, you'd be afraid to go by the pen if you insult those pigs by giving them away like that. No, I'll tell you what, I'll start at double that figure, £14. Yes, that's some sense anyway. Thank you sir, and you sir, yes, we are getting on well, but don't forget those pigs are watching and they won't be satisfied with any nonsense. Well done sir, £16, that's another £17 and another £18. Thank you £19. Any advance on £19, that's right £20." (A pause) " Now come along, it's pork I'm selling not donkey, good for some of you anyway, sorry gentlemen please excuse my levity but we must pay for quality as well as quantity and here is 'pork.' Ah! I thought you would recognise it, that's right £21, now another £22 and £23. Yes, good, now it's against you in the corner, yes I saw you wink £24 and you sir, yes, £25, good. Now have you all done at £25. Ah! I was sure you would not let it go like that. Now another £26, that's right sir. Now it's against you again, you'll not let it go of course, no I know you better than that. Well now have you all done at £26 for these three fine hogs? I shall bang the book if you are not quick. Yes, that's right, £27, now another for you sir, £28, and you sir, over there on the outside ring. Ah! I thought you would like to be in this. Now then once more, have you all finished? Right then, here goes. Ah! £29." But the bid came for £30. " Ah! That's right, I know you want these fine hogs but so does the other fellow, so now it's again against you for the last time and bang goes the book. Mr. G. at £30" (this to the Clerk).

Harry turned away satisfied the price was well above the reserve and would meet the commission and expense.

. . . Away from the noise and the dirt to the cool yard of the *Perkins Arms*, he washed his cart and folded the net. Now for a cup of tea and then to the office for the cheque.

From *Overheard in the Essex Country in the Early 90s*
by A. D. Robertson, 1969.

BE PREPARED!

Directions
By John Bristow, of Ratcliff-Highway,
Engine Maker,
For keeping the largest Size ENGINES with SUCTION
in order, viz.

WHEN the Engine is hard to Work, pull up the Board which hath my name on it, also lift up the little Board at the Bottom, by the Staples, and Oil the insides of the Barrels when the Forces are down; Oil the Chains, and both Ends of the Spindle or Pevets; and if the Chains become slack, take the fork Key and screw up a square Nut on the Top of the Forces, till they are Tight: When needful take off the Carriage Wheels, Grease the Axle-Tree Ends. When it hath play'd very much dirty Water, play clear Water, that the Engine may be cleans'd. Grease the Elbow Screws with Tallow, and do not screw them too hard on, neither screw them off, but screw the Branch off only, because the Leather Pipe, when used, screws on to that Place . . . When the Pipes are not likely to be used for some Time, let all the Water drain out; and after they are dry, coil them up, and hang them in a dry Place: Before they are used again, Liquor them with Neats-Foot-Oyl and Tallow at least once a Year. Some Men may work the Engine with their Hands and others with their Feet; but take a full Stroke from the Top to the Bottom: When you use it to Water Gardens, fix the Fan to the End of the Branch, and the Water will diffuse itself like Gentle Showers . . .

Paint the inside of the Cistern once in two years in Order to preserve it.

From *The Fire Office*
by Bernard Drew, 1952.

NIGHT WATCH

MEN who go out night watching with keepers should not only be perfectly sober when they start, but should also be prohibited from taking any beer with them. I never put much faith in the pluck of a man who was in the habit of taking overmuch beer; there are occasions when a glass of beer does a man good, but it should be taken after he has finished work. Men who come to work boozed, and keep up the booze whilst on duty, are only a nuisance to you, because, if they attempt night watching when full of beer, they are heavy and drowsy, and, directly they sit quietly down in the hut, go off to sleep.

One night I went down the wood to my men at the hut, between ten and eleven at night, and there I found an empty two-gallon jar of beer, whilst the men, five or six in number, lay about fast asleep. I struck a light and called to them, but all the answer I could get was a loud and continuous snore.

From *The Autobiography of an English Gamekeeper, John Wilkins.*
Edited by A. H. Byng and S. M. Stephens, 1892.

SHRIMPING

THE inhabitants of Leigh are nearly all fishermen and their vessels, which are called bawleys, are . . . a very pretty sight to see . . . starting off in the grey of the morning, or coming home in the afternoon w th their shrimps boiling, or being packed all ready for market . . . They boil their shrimps while under weigh, each vessel carrying a copper for the purpose; and the shrimps as soon as caught are cast into a seething cauldron of strong brine—salt water with lumps of salt dissolved in it. This makes the shrimp dry and crisp, and imparts that special salt flavour which makes him harmonise so well with tea and watercress . . .

From *Swin, Swale and Swatchway*
by H. Lewis Jones.

Section 8

IN TIME OF WAR

ROYAL FIGHTIN' TALK

Queen Elizabeth I addressing her troops at Tilbury in 1588 at the time when England faced the threat of invasion from Spain.

"LET tyrants fear; I have always so behaved myself that, under God, I have placed my chiefest strength and safeguard in the loyal hearts and good will of my subjects; and therefore I am come amongst you, as you see, at this time, not for my recreation and disport, but being resolved, in the midst and heat of the battle, to live or die amongst you all, to lay down for my God, and for my kingdoms, and for my people, my honour and my blood, even in the dust.

"I know I have the body of a weak and feeble woman, but I have the heart and stomach of a King, and a King of England too; and think foul scorn that Parma or Spain, or any prince of Europe, should dare to invade the borders of my realm, to which, rather than any dishonour should grow by me, I myself will take up arms, I myself will be your general, judge and rewarder of every one of your virtues in the field."

From *Royalty in Essex*
published by the Essex County Council, 1953.

THE MANNER OF HANDLING . . . ARMS

WHEN the corporals have been through the ranks to see whether their carbines and pistols be charged and they are all ready, then proceed after this manner.

First command silence, then say leisurely and with a distinct voice:

Lay your hands upon your swords.
Draw your swords.

Put your swords into your bridle hands.
Lay your hands upon your carbines.
Advance your carbines.
Cock your carbines.
Present your carbines.
Give fire.
Let fall your carbines.
Lay your hands upon your pistols.
Draw your pistols.
Cock your pistols.
Hold up your hands.
Give fire.

Note:

They must hold up their hands till the word of command be given to:

Return your pistols.

The same words of command are given for the other pistol.

Take your swords from your bridle hands.
Return your swords.

All which motions the officers must take care to see done exactly at the same time for the better grace of the exercising, and therefore must not give the words of command too fast.

From *English History from Essex Sources*
by A. C. Edwards, 1952.

THAT SWEET ENEMY FRANCE . . .

In the troublous times when war with France and the horrors of the French Revolution were creating a fear of invasion in this country . . . steps were taken in Essex to raise local troops and . . . make preparation to repel the enemy, should he effect a landing on these shores. A crack corps of volunteers, the Essex Light Dragoons, was raised by Montague Burgoyne at his own expense in 1796; in addition there were troops of Yeomanry, Cavalry, and Companies of Volunteer Infantry; in almost every parish a corps numbering from 40 to 100 was raised.

Lord Petre marshalled his tenantry with many householders from Brentwood, Ingatestone and neighbouring parishes, and formed them into infantry corps with two bodies of pioneers provided with carriages, horses, drivers and implements—Sir William Hillary of Danbury Park raised the Essex Legion which consisted of 1,000 men including a troop of cavalry from the Dengie Hundred. In the midst of their enthusiasm, however, there was occasionally heard a growl of dissatisfaction—pacifists were to be found even in those days.

Food prices were soaring (a quarten loaf cost 1s. 10½d.) and many were living in a state of destitution and starvation, and consequently it was urged that negotiations for peace should be commenced—but the advocates of submission were overwhelmed by their more courageous countrymen. Schemes of resistance approaching the desperate were adopted by the Government. The Essex Coast was guarded by ten large men-of-war, two brigs and two gunboats. It was resolved that if the invader should succeed in effecting a landing, he should be left to march through a desert—through farms without food or fodder—towns without shelter or inhabitants—to find desolated lands and burning houses.

Accordingly at a meeting of the Deputy Lieutenants of the County held in April, 1798, Lord Braybrooke, as Lord Lieutenant, communicated the following plan he had received from the Secretary of State for driving off the live stock and rendering the inhabitants instrumental in general defence:—

" If an enemy should land upon our shores every possible exertion should be made immediately to deprive him of the means of subsistence. The Navy will soon cut off his communication with the sea, the Army will confine him on shore in such a way as to make it impossible for him to draw any supplies from the adjacent country. In this situation he will be forced to lay down his arms or to give battle on such disadvantageous terms as can leave no doubt of his being defeated.

" In clearing the country the first principle is an indemnification from the Community at large to the individuals for the value of all stock which may be removed in consequence of invasion, if not restored to the respective owners, as also for whatever moveable property may be destroyed by our own arms to prevent its falling into the hands of the Enemy . . ."

The country was accordingly organised for this work and Essex awaited the foe. In the short deceptive peace of 1802 the country began hurriedly to lay down its arms—the Militia were disbanded, the volunteers retired and the camps were broken up. The peaceful calm was of short duration; scarcely had the peasant returned to his plough or the workman to his normal occupation than the war was resumed with fresh fury and the spectre of invasion again haunted Essex. The Militia . . . were again embodied—the volunteer cavalry re-formed, and the infantry man re-armed with his musket or pitchfork.

From *Lords Lieutenants and Keepers of the Rolls of the County of Essex*
by Col. Sir Richard B. Colvin, K.C.B., C.B., T.D., B.A., 1934.

THE LION'S ROAR

In the early hours of May 10 1915, L 38, commanded by Hauptmann Erich Linnarz, made an attack on Southend, but a salvo of unexpected gunfire forced him to take cover beyond Canvey Island. Although Linnarz was lionized, given the hero treatment in Berlin, he was something of a posturing martinet; if a story that has been told, retold, and revised time and time again is to be believed. According to the version that seems to stand up to the various time brackets, he was so enraged by this hostile reception, that after he ordered his helmsman to take L 38 to a higher level, he took an engraved calling card from his wallet, and scrawled on it:

"You English! We have come and
we will come again soon,
to kill or cure!

LINNARZ."

From *The Zeppelin Fighters*
by Arch Whitehouse, 1968.

A SELECT LOT

" GAWD bless my soul! " ejaculated Regimental-Sergeant-Major Cooper, an incarnation of the standardised British version of the great god Mars, as he surveyed his flock of lambs on the parade ground behind the barracks. " Don't know what the Army is coming to now-a-days. Look at that little lot of adjectival sewers. How's a mortal man ever going to turn *them* into soldiers. Well, I s'pose you've got to take it or leave it . . ."

In Colchester the 10th Essex found its true spiritual home. It was not merely that the ancient town was a friendly home country for the regiment, nor that the place was full of memories and traditions of the famous regular units in whose steps we were seeking to follow. But in a benign atmosphere the conglomeration of human flotsam which emergency had thrown together, first gained that corporate spirit that soldiers know as " esprit de corps." It arrived a rabble mob, it marched out as fine as promising a Battalion as any of the great Captains of History could have wished to number in their armies.

From *With the 10th Essex in France*
by Lt.-Col. T. M. Banks and Capt. R. A. Chell, 1924.

OVER THE TOP!—1916

ABOUT 7.20 a.m. our hurricane bombardment became a veritable whirlwind. All our lighter artillery and Stokes' mortars played to their utmost on the front line and close-support trenches of the enemy system. This was the first time Stokes' mortars had been used " all-out," and their effect was at least spectacular; the air was full of toppling and turning cylinders at various stages of flight. And yet other noises and excitements were in store for us in that 10 minutes which preceded our zero hour. At 2 minutes to zero our tunnellers blew strongly charged mines below the old minefield on our right front and below " Kasino Point," slightly to our left; sappers simultaneously blew the charges to open the Russian saps they had made in preceding weeks, as communication trenches with the enemy front line. Kasino Point filled the air around us with lumps of chalk of varying sizes, and a fair number of our men were injured by them. Our little shack was on the trench level, and was quite open on the west side. Several hunks came into this den, and the colonel's servant, Hodges, who was standing at the opening, was almost stunned. He suffered badly from concussion for the rest of the day.

As soon as the mines went up the assaulting troops went over the top, and halted for a few seconds to get their line straight. The barrage lifted, and forward they all went with cheers and yells straight for the Hun. The line 100 yards away was invisible for a time—there was so much smoke.

From *With the 10th Essex in France*
by Lt.-Col. T. M. Banks and Capt. R. A. Chell, 1924.

MALDON EXPECTS . . .

THE Parish Invasion Committee has made preliminary plans in collaboration with the Military Authorities to deal as far as possible with the various problems which will arise in invasion conditions, e.g., casualties, feeding, housing and sheltering the homeless, repair of roads, etc.

Everyone, man, woman and older child, can help and all must play their part in beating the invader.

If you do not yet know how your services can best be utilized, or are in need of advice to meet any personal difficulties, consult the Committee at once. Above all carry on your ordinary work as long as possible if this is essential to the life of the community

and STAND FIRM.

From *Warmen Courageous*
by Peter Finch, 1951.

ENEMY RAIDERS APPROACHING

THE most impressive war sight I have yet seen in the sky in daylight was just before the beginning of the big London blitz in September.

It was about five in the evening, I think, and I was ironing on a big table out in the yard. The hum of planes, which by this time had become a commonplace, was in the air but I was not taking much notice of it until it grew and grew until I felt it rather than heard it beating on my eardrums. Then I looked up and saw in the mid-sky over the apple-store seventy-five Junkers bombers in formation. They came sailing along, low enough to see and apparently very slowly. It was an incredibly menacing sight . . . There were a few high clouds in the sky and against their goose-breasts the planes looked black and enormous.

I shouted to Cliff, who had paused by the gate on one of his trips up the village, and he said, " No, no, they're ours. Must be."

I said, " I don't think we've got that many, have we? " for I had not done counting and was frightened and therefore irritated with him.

I saw two little planes darting in and out amongst them, moving up and down like a woman sewing, for quite a while, or it seemed a while, until they began to break formation, and then I realised who and what the little ones were. It did not look real, any of it. And then, over the house . . . the whole armada of them slowly swung round and sailed out to sea again . . .

When it was all over and the last drone of the engines had died, Christine brought me a tin hat and made me wear it while I finished the ironing . . .

From *The Oaken Heart*
by Margery Allingham, 1941.

HOME GUARD

" . . . So here's to the Old Boys who answered the Call
Forgetting their ages, rheumatics and all;
Who dared Hitler's might and awaited the Hun
With nought but stout hearts and a twelve-bore gun."

A VIVID picture of the early months of the Home Guard comes from Colonel Hughes's pen:

"In July, August and September of 1940, the Home Guard

regarded itself as on duty all the time. Every man asked himself—‘ What shall I do if a —— German suddenly drops from the skies outside my house, office or workshop door? ’ And because it was a practical possibility many took rifles to work with them, especially if they worked in the country. In the same way their wives prepared for a similar contingency in the same spirit—no cup of tea and cigarette, but a handful of pepper and the carving knife!

“ And of the long hours spent in observation posts or at Company or Platoon Headquarters, little was wasted. When it was an important duty to keep watch for enemy landings over wide stretches of countryside where planes or gliders would meet little opposition, observation posts were established overlooking Bulphan Fen, Pitsea Marshes, Mucking Flats and the Tilbury Marshes. Many a man spent long nights in lonely places in 1940 and 1941, but never alone; and the man resting, remembering his normal day's work to perform when he went off duty, slept every minute he could snatch. At Platoon Headquarters, officer or sergeant seized the opportunity to issue clothing or equipment to members of the nightly guard, to collect particulars for a new nominal roll complete with some unheard-of detail and to perfect recruits in the rules of aiming, the best way to cripple tanks, the art of clearing a wood of the enemy, or the duties of a sentry. When the hour's instruction had ended the tea was brewed, sandwiches eaten and the latest news of home and battlefield chewed and digested. Then most laid down and slept until their turn of duty came. One of the rest produced a well-thumbed pack of cards, and in a little pool of light around a candle, a few heads were bent over a game of brag or pontoon.”

From *Warmen Courageous*
by Peter Finch, 1951.

THAMES-SIDE GUARDIANS

AFTER a breakfast of Southend dabs and fried mushrooms from the marshes, I went on, on that early morning of the last painful year of war, to Canvey, the isle that the Phœnicians knew, the isle which for six long years was alive with the guns that guarded London's seaways . . .

In a green field bright with brassy kingcups, daisies, and cuckoo flowers, there squatted an anti-aircraft site. Another crouched nearer the sea-wall.

At a point high on the near mainland by the ruins of Hadleigh Castle, from whose gaunt keep smugglers, a century ago, flashed their signal lights to their comrades nosing up the creeks, was another battery. Its guns swept the skies as the questing nose of a dog will read the wind for news of game.

One looked out over thousands of acres of green and shining marsh to the wide and glittering estuary. Merchantmen, each of whom had dared and won his part in the Battle of the Atlantic, came in on the tide.

" When I first came here," said the quiet voice of the young Canadian major, who commanded these outposts, " I thought we would not see much shipping coming up Old Father Thames. But some days I've seen ships come in in a regular procession—right fine to see them go by. It's a great lesson to those who want to know what the Navy is doing."

He was thirty-two, the " granddaddy " of this battery, whose average age of both officers and men was between twenty-three and twenty-five. They ranged from nineteen to thirty, with four or five veterans of forty who caught the tag end of the last war.

From the moment the predictor plotted the approaching 'plane to the instant the gun was fired only a few seconds elapsed. Yet thirty-three men each played their part in that fraction of time.

First, the 'plane was spotted; then the predictor plotted its course and gave it to the firing-room, the firing-room telephoned range, height and speed to the gun.

The guns swept sky or estuary with equal ease. They could bring down a bomber or sink a destroyer. They fired ten rounds a minute; but if dive-bombers attacked they threw up a " diver barrage " of thirty to forty shots a minute.

Their accuracy of fire was uncanny. I have talked with many fighter and bomber pilots who had been on daylight sweeps over Northern France and mass bombing raids on Germany. They confirmed what the gunners believed—that the Germans disposed many times more guns and searchlights than we did, but that their accuracy of fire was not comparable to ours. The French coast was girdled by a bank of searchlights twenty miles in depth—yet night after night our bombers got through.

Compare this with what happened on the island and its mainland when the big blitz was on. One civilian was killed and a few were wounded. No troops lost their lives. One gun-site on Canvey fired over a thousand rounds in a week.

" There was tharty o' them owd Jarman bombers come oover us one night alone," said a local fishermen, shaking his grey head reminiscently. " Me and the missus counted 'em. The guns was a-gooin' off like one o'clock. They fair shook the hull island. Them owd Jarmans was a-comin' down right and left like ducks. There warn't one on 'em got back to Jarmany that night . . . "

Imagine yourself for a moment here on a moon-misty night in this late spring of war. Curlew call on the saltings, and the bar-geese laugh their ghastly mirth out on the mud—that chilling laugh which all old fishermen tell you is the ghosts of dead sailors, jeering at those about to follow them by drowning. The cattle lie humped in the fields, scattered islets in a silver sea of mist.

In the concrete firing-room tin-hatted youngsters, brown as berries, serious-eyed, listen intently at telephones, pore over the plotting table. Staccato words and phrases are rapped out. The predictor people call down angles and heights—" Six thousand." " Set six thousand," snaps the control officer. A code word is called. Quadrant elevation, time of flight and length of fuse follow.

At the guns other telephones snap commands, repeat them.

Somewhere out in the moon-haze a great black Ju.88, loaded with sea-mines, swoops low over the estuary like a ghastly night-hawk.

" Fire! "

Tongues of flame sear the half-light, the reports thud through the riven silence. A mile out over the dark water the shells burst, red and yellow flowers in the night.

Other reports thud forth, other shells whine out and burst. The black nighthawk, caught in a withering blast of splinters and concussion, lurches. A shell strikes it fair and square. Its mine-load explodes with a shattering detonation. Bits and pieces of fuselage, wings, struts and men rain down into the water. Another one is in the bag.

That is a lucky night. There were nights when they came in from the sea to be caught in such a withering blast of fire that, although it could not be known for certain whether they were badly hit or not, they were forced to turn tail and flee.

Most nights they came singly or in fours, but there was a night when fourteen came into the mouth of the Thames and were put to flight. Some nights there were as many as thirty. There was little sleep and no easy living for these men.

From *Coastal Adventure* by J. Wentworth Day, 1949.

1941—AN EVENTFUL YEAR

THE New Year came in . . .

The winter, though not comparable to the previous one, was bitter . . . January 31 was a day of low cloud . . . The previous day a plane had been brought down on the marshes near St. Osyth.

Abbott's Hall Farm, Wigborough, was at this time claimed by Mr. J. Mortimer to be " the most bombed farm in Essex."

Fire-watching was now coming into its own, though still not on a compulsory basis . . . In February the Chairman of Colchester Fire Brigade Committee called for 10,000 volunteers by March 1.

British Restaurants were now in the making. The Mayor of Colchester ate his first ninepenny dinner on May 20 in the strangely located restaurant in Ind Coope's Brewery, East Hill.

February 24 saw an attack on Harwich which went on for two hours, filling the sky with gun flashes, searchlights and flares.

On March 8 residents of Gosbecks Road, Shrub End, were going to bed when an H.E. bomb fell in a garden there . . .

The following extracts from a diary kept at the time can best suggest the pace of this period in the Colchester area.

" March 19. Big raid on London docks. Thousands of 'planes going over the town all night.

" March 22. New invasion notices posted, urging immediate evacuation of old people, children, etc.

" April 2. Some cows at St. Osyth got out through the wire and exploded several mines. The noise very loud . . .

" April 17. Duke of Gloucester passed through the town about 6 o'clock, going towards Ipswich, travelling very fast. There was an Army camouflaged car, then another flying a General's flag, then a dark-coloured Rolls, and lastly 2 M.P.s on motor-cycles.

" April 13. Rumours going round the town tonight that an invasion is imminent.

" April 21. Tremendous damage done on Saturday night at Ilford, Chadwell Heath, Stratford and the eastern suburbs. Whole line blocked, and yesterday London trains were being sent round the Dunmow line and through Bishop's Stortford.

" May 1. Duchess of Gloucester in the town, inspecting the Red Cross depot at the library.

" May 9. Bombs on works at Chelmsford; several killed. Also at Clacton, where two big bombs fell in the main street, but nobody hurt there.

" May 23. No raids for four nights.

" May 31. Notices put up in the Banks yesterday, advising all customers able to do so to remove their accounts or valuables to branches in safer areas.

" June 14. Most definite rumours tonight of an invasion within 24 hours. A.R.P. people certainly believe it for a fact.

" July 28. At 4.30 a.m. German 'plane shot down by a night fighter. Passed over the town and fell near some cottages at Wivenhoe Park.

" August 6. Two land mines late tonight, near Collier's Wood, Ardleigh. Slight damage to farm buildings . . .

" Nov. 3. Gas exhibition at the Castle. A lecturer said: ' It is not a matter of "if" the Germans use gas at Colchester; it is simply a question of " when." ' Several A.R.P. officers who attended forgot to bring their own respirators.

" Nov. 27. At about 7 p.m. a German 'plane flew low over the town and dropped a couple of mines near Bromley...

' Dec. 6. Grand invasion manœuvres. Everybody ordered off the streets . . .

" Dec. 20. An attack on aerodromes at 5.45 p.m. in a thick fog. Two mines dropped near Panfield Hall, damaging windows and roof."

From *Essex at War*
edited by Hervey Benham, 1945.

ORDERS IS ORDERS!

One of the very last orders given to the 1st Battalion, The Essex Regiment, before entraining to the forward areas of Eastern India and Burma in 1944:

" ATTENTION is drawn to the fact that women members of the U.S.A. Forces are not allowed to marry without first obtaining the approval of the Commanding General U.S. Forces, China, Burma and India. Before contracting a marriage with a woman member of the U.S.A. Forces, any officer or other rank will therefore make sure that permission has been obtained."

From *The Essex Regiment, 1929-1950*
by Col. T. A. Martin, 1952.

Section 9

KEEPING THE PEACE

THE POLICEMAN'S LOT

THE law requires, and the public demand, that every Constable should be *idoneus homo*. He must be sober, honest, healthy, capable, prompt in action, courteous, and possess a certain amount of legal knowledge; in fact, be a very competent all-round man . . . he should execute the office without malice, affection or partiality; knowledge to understand what he ought to do; and ability, as well in substance or estate as in body, to enable him to conduct himself with utility to the public.

From *A Short History of the Essex Constabulary*
by Barnett Tabrum, 1911.

A MUSCULAR DETERRENT

From a Petition prepared in July, 1645, of the Constables and Inhabitants of Walthamstow to the Justices requesting provision of Stocks and Whipping Post for the Treatment of Offenders.

> THE humble peticion of the constabelles and other of the inhabitantes of the parish of Walthamstow in the . . . County . . .

Humbly shewing that in the parish of Walthamstow there is at this present: neyther a payer of stockes: nor a whipping post: which by the Law ought to be in every parish within this kingdom: the very sight whereof might be: a means to keep som from offending the Law: a means for the execution of the Law upon others: for want whereof the said constabelles cannot punnish offenders according to the Law: And therfore desiere an Order from this honorabell Court that there may be a payer of stockes and a whipping post provided within the said parish . . .

. . . .

The Order of the Court is added to the petition and reads:

. . . That the Constables at the charge of the inh(abi)tants of the towne shall within one moneth sett upp the stocks and a whippinge post, and the Lord of the Mannor to sett upp a pillery and provide such other things as by lawe he ough(t) to provide . . .

From *The Quarter Sessions Records—The Essex Record Office.*

OF ROGUES AND VAGABONDS

By Statute 17 George II chap. 25 (commonly called the Vagrant Act), together with other statutes dating back to Elizabeth, it was ordered that " Justices should meet in their respective divisions four times in the year or oftener, to have every parish searched for rogues or vagabonds."

According to Burns's " Justice of the Peace," 1797, those who should be deemed such included " persons going about as patent gatherers, or gathering alms, under pretences of loss by fire, or other casualty. Persons going about as collectors for prisons, gaols, or hospitals. Fences, or receivers of stolen properties. Bearwards, or itinerant owners of performing animals. Common players of interludes, and all persons who shall for hire, gain or reward, act, represent, or perform any interlude, tragedy, comedy, opera, play, farce, or other entertainment of the stage, not being authorised by law. Minstrels and Jugglers. All persons pretending to be gipsies, or wandering in the habit or form of Egyptians. Pretending to have skill in physiognomy, palmistry, or like crafty service, or to tell fortunes. Using any subtel craft to deceive or impose on any of his Majesty's subjects. Playing or betting at any unlawful games or plays. All persons who run away and leave their wives or children chargeable to the parish. All petty chapmen or pedlars wandering abroad, not being duly licensed. All persons wandering abroad, and lodging in alehouses, barnes, out-houses, or in the open air, and not giving a good account of themselves. All persons begging and pretending to be soldiers, mariners, or sea-faring men, and not being licensed to do so by a Justice of the Peace, or anyone pretending to leave his parish to go to work in harvest, unless he have a certificate from the Minister or one churchwarden where he resides, that he hath a house or dwelling place there."

A reward of two shillings was to be given to anyone apprehending such and handing him over to the parish constable. The Justice of the Peace shall order such persons to be publicly whipped or imprisoned in the common gaol.

From *The Hundred of Beacontree—a Police Division of Essex.*
by William Tyler, 1925.

THE COUNTY'S FIRST POLICE CHIEF

At the General Quarter Session of the Peace holden by adjournment at Chelmsford in and for the County of Essex on Tuesday the 11th day of February 1840 . . . It is ordered by this Court that Captain John Bunch Bonnemaison McHardy of the Royal Navy . . . is hereby appointed Chief Constable of the said County . . .

From *The Quarter Sessions Records—The Essex Record Office.*

FORMING THE FORCE

Notes from a Report prepared by the Committee appointed by the Court of Quarter Session to confer with the Chief Constable and consider the best means for carrying out the provisions of the Rural Police Act.

1. . . . Superintendents . . . should be provided with Horses the better to enable them to perform the duties of their office

. . . the Chief Constable having the assistance of a veterinary Surgeon and . . . that 2/- per day shall be allowed to each Superintendent for forage.

2. The Committee also recommend that a sample of Sadlery be procured for the use of the superintendents . . .

3. The Committee directed the Chief Constable to apply to the persons supplying the Metropolitan Police with Clothing and ascertain whether they would supply the clothing for the whole force for this County on the same terms . . .

4. The Committee recommend the same description of Great Coats for the Superintendents and Constables as those used by the Metropolitan Police and that on the Collar of the Coat there shall be marked the Crown and number and on the button the words Essex Constabulary with an impression of the County.

5. That a sufficient number of Truncheons bearing the County arms shall be procured at 7/6 each . . .

6. The Committee further report that they are of opinion that the Constabulary Force will be rendered much more efficient if it be located in certain parts of the County and if Lock-up houses and Guard Rooms are provided . . .

7. The Committee also recommend that one Light Cart and Harness for one Horse be provided for each station where a Superintendent shall be placed . . .

8. . . . the Committee recommend the Court to allow the Chief Constable a Secretary for the first year . . . at a salary of £100 for the year.

From *The Essex Record Office.*

THE MOAT FARM MURDER

RICKLING itself, which lies at some distance from the Green, would not delay any visitor unless he were morbid; but if he were, then he would relish the knowledge that Rickling is the nearest village within range of what was once called " the Moat Farm." He will not have forgotten, if true to type, the Moat Farm Murder which came as so great a boon to newspaper proprietors in 1903. And, as murders go, this murder was remarkable.

Miss Camille Cecile Holland was, at the age of fifty-six, living in London with a pleasant income to support her. She wrote mild verses and painted mild water-colours. And in 1898 she met, at the Earl's Court Exhibition, a cheerful anthropoid named Samuel Herbert Dougal. He had been a good soldier for some twenty-three years, but by this time had left the army. Unfortunately he had lost his pension when he was convicted of forgery. Well, astonishingly enough, he managed to make Miss Holland his mistress, and together they set up house at the Moat Farm. Dougal, however, had no intention of becoming a farmer. He meant to live upon Miss Holland's money; and one day, finding that she resented his playfulness with the servant-girl, he took her for a drive, not in his " locomobile " (as he called it), but in the trap. Then, near the end of his little domain, he shot her behind the ear—apparently at a time when she was not looking; so perhaps the poor woman has never realised that she was murdered. Dougal immediately buried her body in a handy ditch; and within a few days he had caused the ditch to be filled in. After this, he lived cheerfully for another four years, imposing upon Miss Holland's bank by sending letters and cheques in a forged hand . . .

But in 1902 there was so much gossip at Clavering that the local police became interested. They even began to dig in the moat and, under instructions from Scotland Yard, more successfully, in the ditch. They next made enquiries at Miss Holland's bank, wondering how she could have drawn money if, as Dougal assured them, she was not in England. They arrested the hearty Dougal and he was imprisoned at Chelmsford. While he was awaiting his trial he wrote several genial letters . . . but in spite of so much bonhomie, Dougal went to the gallows.

From *Highways and Byways in Essex*
by Clifford Bax, 1939.

Section 10

THE QUEEN'S HIGHWAY

KEEPING WATCH

A note from the records of the Epiphany Session of the Essex Quarter Sessions, 1642-1643.

To the right honourable and right worshipfull his Majestie's Justices of the peace within the County of Essex now assembled att their generall Session . . .

The humble Peticion of the Inhabitants of Chadwell ward in the parish of Barking . . .

Showeth

That the peticioners have been lately enforced to keepe a stronge watch neere the Whaleboane in the greate roade neere Romford by reason of sundry greate robberies there lately committed.

That the constable and watchmen there attending in the night beinge farr from shelter are exposed to the violenes of stormes tempest and could to the greate hazard of their healths.

There humble suite to this honourable Court is that the Court wilbe pleased to order that a watch house may be erected in some convenient place mor neere the said high waie for the shelter of the said watch, and that the money to be disbursed for the same may be levyed and raised by a rate and assessment upon the several habitants of the same ward . . .

From *The Essex Record Office.*

A PERILOUS UNDERTAKING

In the early part of the eighteenth century travelling was very unpleasant and insecure. The highways were in a wretched condition; and though it is stated a great improvement in them commenced in the time of George II; so recently as 1795 we read of seven loaded wagons remaining stuck fast, sunk up to their axletrees, in the great trunk road between Ingatestone and Chelmsford—a distance of six miles. A journey from the heart of the county was a matter that required serious thought and a week's preparation; and we find it advertised as an extraordinary feat, and not without some apologetic explanations to allay the terror of the public at the peril of the undertaking, that " flying machines "—a sort of cross between the wagon and the stage coach, drawn by chain traces—would leave Chelmsford at eight or nine o'clock in the morning, and actually reach London the same night, returning on the following morning; thus, by extra exertion, accomplishing in two days, and at enormous expense, a journey which may now be performed by a return ticket, in a second-class carriage, for 7s. 6d., in less than three hours.

From *The People's History of Essex*
by D. W. Coller, 1861.

NO PAVEMENT OF DIAMONDS—NO STREETS OF GOLD

Of all the cursed roads which ever disgraced this kingdom, in the very ages of barbarism, none ever equalled that from *Billericay* to the *King's-head* at *Tilbury*. It is for near 12 miles so narrow, that a mouse cannot pass by any carriage . . . The rutts are of an incredible depth—and a pavement of diamonds might as well be sought for as a quarter. The trees everywhere over-grow the road, so that it is totally impervious to the sun, except at a few places: And to add to all the infamous circumstances, which concur to plague a traveller, I must not forget the eternally meeting with chalk-waggons; themselves frequently stuck fast, till a collection of them are in the same situation, and twenty or thirty horses may be tacked to each, to draw them out one by one . . .

From *A Six Weeks Tour Through the Southern Counties . . .*
by Arthur Young, 1771.

MAINTAINING THE HIGHWAY

NOTHING can more clearly evidence the value and importance of good roads, than the great improvements to which of late years they have so much contributed . . . In many parts of the county the difficulty and expense of procuring proper materials for making good roads, is very great; but even in those places (and although the materials may cost from one-penny to three-half-pence a bushel, and the road rates upon the rack rents being occasionally from three to four shillings in the pound) the exertions of the parishioners are unceasing, seeing that their health, comfort, and convenience, are so much dependent thereon.

From *A General View of Agriculture in the County of Essex*
by Charles Vancouver, 1795.

THE CARD

THE ordinary citizen can have little sympathy with burglars and thieves, but occasionally there is one so resourceful and funny we have to laugh admiringly at his exploits and say that he really was a " card." Such a " card " was Stephen Bunce, who was hanged at Tyburn in 1707.

On one occasion he was walking along the road near Romford when he saw a gentleman coming towards him on a fine horse. Stephen Bunce immediately lay down in the middle of the road until the gentleman came up.

" What are you lying down there like that for? " asked the gentleman.

" Ssh! " ordered Bunce, raising a solemn forefinger.

" What on earth are you listening to? " shouted the gentleman.

" Oh," said Bunce, " I never expected to hear fairies. This is the loveliest music I have heard in all my life, and I never expect to hear such music again."

The gentleman, anxious not to miss such an unusual treat, jumped down from his horse and threw the reins to Bunce to hold. While the gentleman was pressing his ear to the road, Bunce mounted the horse and rode off at great speed to Romford. The gentleman who had been left behind listening for fairy music was a Mr. Bartlett, who was well known in Romford, and his horse made its way to an inn which was well used by his master. The ready-witted Bunce said that Mr. Bartlett was busy gambling at Ingatestone and needed fifteen guineas, for which he had been instructed to leave the horse as a pledge. The fifteen guineas were handed over and Bunce departed as speedily as possible.

Some hours later Mr. Bartlett arrived on foot, and the inn-keeper met him with the words, " Why did you bother to send your horse as a pledge? I would have advanced the fifteen guineas without hesitation." What Mr. Bartlett said was not recorded.

From *Essex Blood and Thunder*
by George Caunt, 1967.

THE NIGHT MAIL—1818

In the spring of 1785 the first mail coaches ran in Essex, supplanting the post boys on their horses. These became the aristocrats of public coaches: they were fast and ran to a carefully planned and rigidly enforced timetable. The Norwich to London mail coach in 1818, for example, was to leave Norwich at 4 p.m. each day, reaching Newmarket by 11, Quendon by 2.15, Harlow by 4, and the General Post Office in the City at 7 next morning... By the 1820s there were many coaches, besides the mail coaches, on regular runs on Essex roads. Every day some twenty of them, with names like the *Norwich Phenomenon*, the *Colchester Eclipse* and the *Chelmsford Ship*, travelled up and down Chelmsford High Street on their way from a dozen towns in Essex and East Anglia to London and back again, gay in green, yellow or blue.

These were the 'buses of the day.

From *Highways and Byways of Essex*—
the Essex County Council, 1955.

THE COLCHESTER MACHINE

. . . until our meal was ready, we had the fun of watching the Colchester mail-coach arrive. Its name is quite rightly the Colchester

Machine, seating six people inside, in front outside behind the coachman four more, and at the back, where the trunks usually go, as many again within a neat enclosure with benches, while eight people were sitting above on deck, their feet dangling overboard, holding fast with their hands to screwed-in brass rings. This was a new experience for us; we called to each other to come, and my Karl investigated the structure of the machine as soon as it was empty; this took place with all possible convenience to the passengers, as not only those occupying the seats of honour inside were able to descend as in every other good coach, but the rest could climb down too with the aid of small, prettily worked and painted ladders placed alongside, like those found at home in well-appointed libraries. Travellers cannot take many or large parcels with them, though they can manage quite well for themselves alone, as such good roads should not jolt them much. Half an hour after we saw them re-enter, supplied with horses just as good and swift as those on our coach.

Sophie in London
by Sophie La Roche.

From *Essex at Work: 1700-1815*
by A. F. J. Brown, 1969.

THE OWD LANE

OLD Sam Aylett, more familiarly known as "Pudden Aylett," by reason of a certain rotundity of face and figure, paused to glance critically at the brand new signpost recently erected for the benefit of such as might desire to explore by devious and difficult ways certain lesser known parts of the country. The signpost read "Public Footpath to Duck's Croft and Mucking's Green." Sam turned to his companion, Bob Francis, a little old man with a white beard and keen blue eyes, generally known by the name of "Beesey Francis," on account of his skill in the management of bees, and pointed to the signpost.

"Wha's that say on ther' boy?" he enquired. "Me owd eyes ain't s'good as th' used ter was." Bob adjusted a pair of spectacles to his nose and spelt out the contents of the signpost slowly. "P-U-B-L-I-C F-O-O-T-P-A-T-H T-O D-U-C-K-S C-R-O-F-T A-N-D M-U-C-K-I-N-G-S G-R-E-E-N." "Cor," he added, "Muckin' Green! Why ther' ain't nothen there, and ain't bin nit these last forty year n'more. Tha's a proper master ter tell ye ter goo wher' ther' ain't nothen ter goo fur. Dall ut! That owd path ain't bin used fur ter goo th' Muckins way nit fur forty year, I'll lay."

From *The Magic Mawkin and other Essex Tales*
by H. Cranmer-Byng.

A TRACTION ENGINE IN TROUBLE

Part of the report of the District Surveyor to the Hedingham Highway Board in October, 1868:

. . . THE Highway leading from Crows Cross to Halstead was completely blocked near Mr Rist's Saturday the 19th Sept by two carriages laden with timber and drawn by a Traction Engine . . . My attention was called to the fact about 11 o'clock in the forenoon and proceeding to the spot found that it was caused by one of the Timber carriages loaded very heavily having sunk through the surface of the carriageway and into the sand. Several trials were made in my presence to extricate it without avail. The timber had therefore to be unloaded before the carriage could be removed which was not until 11 o'clock at night. The other carriage was left upon the road without any person in charge and remained there until the Monday morning. A man was employed by me during the two nights to remain by it to warn persons in passing. There is no doubt but that the stoppage of this thoroughfare was occasioned by excessive loading and which is contrary to the provisions of the Act 24th and 25th Vic cap 70 sec 4 . . . I estimate the cost of reinstating the road to its former condition at about seven pounds and recommend that the Board institute proceedings . . .

From *The Essex Record Office.*

THOSE WERE THE DAYS!

Of all the various ways of spending a summer holiday, of all the many modes of travel, where pleasure, not speed, is the chief consideration, commend to me a driving tour, with all its charming independence and the exceptional opportunities it affords of leisurely seeing and thoroughly comprehending the rare charms of our beautiful English scenery—scenery of its kind unequalled in the world.

The fortunate traveller by road, how enviable is his lot! He is delivered from the bondage of time-tables, the pleasure of his outing is never marred by weary waiting at dismal junctions, or hurried rushing to catch certain trains—or miss them, as the case may be. Haste and bustle form no part or parcel of his programme: his is rather a quiet, restful progress; being master of his own time, he can rise and breakfast when he likes, can start on his day's journey just when he chooses; he knows nothing of the worry of luggage, for his belongings always go with him, he leaves his hotel door in his own carriage and arrives at his night's destination in like manner. Having full control over his conveyance, he can stop at any spot by the way that may take his fancy, he can loiter or make haste, just as his inclination at the time may dictate—in fine, he travels in the truest sense of the word, he is not simply conveyed from place to place, as is a passenger by railway. An ideal way of spending a summer holiday this surely? Storing one's mind with a gallery of lovely landscapes and beauty-spots, never to be forgotten; acquiring at the same time an intimate knowledge of the rare charms of rural England; gathering pleasant experiences each day, and gaining health and strength besides. What a happy combination of good things!

One of the most attractive features of such a journey is its perfect freedom.

From *A Tour In A Phaeton*
by James John Hissey, 1889.

Section 11

SPORTS AND PASTIMES

A HUNTING HE WILL GO

FEW have investigated more closely than I have done the depth, and breadth, and water-holding capacities of an Essex ditch. It will, I think, be accorded to me by Essex men generally that I have ridden hard. The cause of my delight in the amusement I have never been able to analyse to my own satisfaction. In the know very much of the accessories of the field. I am too blind to see hounds turning, and cannot therefore tell whether the fox has gone this way or that. Indeed all the notice I take of hounds is not first place, even now, I know very little about hunting—though I to ride over them. My eyes are so constituted that I can never see the nature of a fence. I either follow some one, or ride at it with the full conviction that I may be going into a horse-pond or a gravel-pit. I have jumped into both the one and the other. I am very heavy, and have never ridden expensive horses. I am also now old for such work, being so stiff that I cannot get on to my horse without the aid of a block or bank. But I ride still after the same fashion, with a boy's energy, determined to get ahead if it may possibly be done, hating the roads, despising young men who ride them, and with a feeling that life can not, with all her riches, have given me anything better than when I have gone through a long run to the finish, keeping a place, not of glory, but of credit, among my juniors.

From *An Autobiography*
by Anthony Trollope, 1883.

BULL-BAITING

Advertised in the Chelmsford Chronicle *on 30th December, 1784.*

"THIS IS TO GIVE NOTICE TO ALL GENTLEMEN BULL-BAITERS.

THAT there is a Bull to be baited at Mr. Talladay's at the *White Hart*, Maldon, for a Silver Spoon of fourteen shillings value (the dog that runs best of three heats to be entitled to the Spoon) on Wednesday, Old Christmas Day, the 5th day of January, and the second-best dog to be entitled to half-a-crown. The Bull to be at the stake at ten o'clock. Dinner on the table at one o'clock."

It is difficult to guess how the second-best dog decided to spend the half-crown, but easy to picture that boisterous dinner of bloodthirsty Britons at the *White Hart*.

From *Highways and Byways in Essex*
by Clifford Bax, 1939.

BEN CAUNT'S LAST FIGHT

ESSEX had not been a fashionable county for prize fights in earlier times, but with the strengthening of the forces of law and order (magistrates and police, or, as they were known in early Victorian times, beaks and blues) it became difficult to stage a prizefight without the beaks and blues arriving to stop the fight. The promoters of the fights went to great trouble to fool the authorities by laying false trails. It would be announced that a special train would leave, say, King's Cross for the fight, and the special train did leave for an unknown destination, but another special train (unannounced) packed with those "in the know" would start from Fenchurch Street for Tilbury. The passengers would embark on boats specially hired and sail out into the estuary, then double back to a secret destination on the Essex or Kent marshes, where the ring would be rapidly erected.

One of the famous contests on the coast of the Essex estuary was between two veterans who had been friends but had quarrelled. Ben Caunt, who had been champion from 1838 to 1845, had retired to become a prosperous publican and owned the Coach and Horses (now the Salisbury) in St. Martin's Lane. In 1857, as the result of a family feud, Ben Caunt at forty-two and Nat Langham at thirty-seven signed articles to fight. Ben's fighting blood was up, because he issued a challenge to twenty-nine-year-old Tom Sayers to fight for the championship for £200 a side. The Caunt-Langham contest took place on Canvey Island on September 22, 1857. Trains left Fenchurch Street for Tilbury and Southend, and boats were hired to rendezvous at Southend. After some confusion the boats turned sharply back up-river, and the ring was set up and ready at 4.15 p.m. Both men threw their hats into the ring as was the custom and stripped off. They were mighty men of muscle, with bodies like Greek gods, and their battered faces showed that they were veteran boxers. As this was a personal quarrel there was no shaking hands.

After some preliminary sparring, Caunt landed a left and right on Langham's ribs and he went down laughing for the first round. The fight lasted sixty rounds, and Caunt did not go down once, but Langham had been down fifty-nine times. In the fifty-first round Caunt swung a punch with his left which missed Langham but landed on one of the wooden stakes forming the ring. In the sixtieth round they stood and looked at each other and rubbed their chests. Both prizefighters appeared to have had enough, and were persuaded to shake hands and be friends again. This was Ben Caunt's last fight.

From *Essex Blood and Thunder*
by George Caunt, 1967.

MUSIC HATH CHARMS

THE very great Number of Musical Societies, Catch-Clubs, &c. which are now established, both in Town and Country, plainly demonstrate that Part-Songs and Catches, never were so much in Vogue in England, as at present; the Practice of which (if rightly used) may be esteemed as very commendable, not only in its being an innocent Amusement, and a pleasant Evening Recreation, after the burthensome Fatigues of the Day, for Persons to join in Singing of melodious Songs and Catches, that Peace and Tranquility may thereby be introduced into a Neighbourhood, and social Harmony abound, where perhaps before did dwell the greatest Animosities. For

Music hath a powerful Charm,
That can the fiercest Rage disarm:
Calm Passions in a human Breast;
And lull ev'n Jealousy to rest.
So great is Music's Power.

From *The Essex Harmony*
by John Arnold, 1786.

THE PURLEIGH HORNPIPE

ONE of the first village tap-rooms which I made the acquaintance of was at Purleigh, a large parish well away from the railway and supplied with some really admirable specimens of the Essex labourer. It was here that I saw the *Labourer Enjoying Himself.*

When I went into the house I heard a sound of revelry in the "tap," and on going in found there a jovial crew of about sixteen or more labourers, making a tremendous noise, and "driving dull care away" after their hard day's work, with a zeal which I never saw equalled in any other tap-room. They were soon glum enough, however, when they saw a stranger darkening the door . . . I went into the other bar for a short time, and almost as soon as my back was turned the deafening din at once re-commenced. I could hear the sound of music and of dancing, and at the end of a fairly long interval there was a prodigious demonstration of applause from the thick boots and hearty lungs of the gathering. In the bar parlour I found a farm bailiff, who told me that the amusement consisted of the "*Purleigh Hornpipe,*" a dance which was done to the accompaniment of melodion and tambourine. The music and the dance, he said, had been handed down from generation to generation, and the Purleigh labourer never tired of it. Now and then they would vary the dancing with a song, but the hornpipe gave the greatest pleasure . . .

The activity of the dancer and the amazing amount of sound which he got out of the floor and his hob-nailed boots, were the chief features of the performance. There was no rope-pulling or other embellishment, but a plain steady dance of a most exhausting character which went on for a long time, and which was at once taken up by dancer No. 2, when the first had had enough of it, and was glad to repair his energies with some beer, which he fetched very gleefully at my desire . . .

My friend the bailiff assured me that this sort of entertainment went on regularly every night until closing time.

From *The Essex Labourer*
by W. Gurney Benham, 1888.

CYCLING

THE members of the Braintree Bicycle Club had a race a few evenings since, the course being from the Bay Tree Farm to the County Court Office, in the Coggeshall Rd., a distance of about two miles. There were ten starters who were handicapped according to the diameter of the wheels of their machines . . . As soon as the start was effected, a good race was maintained between Beard, Davies and the brothers Crittall as far as Mr. Henry Hobbs'; at that point, however, the two latter moved far ahead of their competitors and raced each other almost neck and neck to the finish, the younger of the two, F. H. Crittall, and captain of the club, just succeeding in winning. The race was witnessed by a large number of spectators.

From *The Halstead Times*, 1877.

WILD-FOWLER

PHILOSOPHERS have told us that nothing comes up to the expectation of it, and perhaps they are right, yet new experiences cannot be gained from expectation; that is certain sure. On the other hand, a great deal of pleasure may be found in the thoughts of past nights and days, living those morning and evening flights in retrospect, and stretching the imagination to times and tides which are beyond any direct or settled expectations.

Thus, I stand again beside a favourite little creek from which the tide is flowing, leaving on either bank those muds which, at a distance, become less mud than saltings, until as the patches of marram-grass and sea-lavender grow wider and closer, forming eventually a compact mass of cover intersected by numerous small creeks and gutters, the saltings proper take shape, stretching away to the shining muds of the estuary.

Slowly, how slowly, my creek becomes empty, the waters draining from it at its own slovenly pace. I am unable to cross to the muds opposite until only a few inches of water remain. I am reminded of the proverbial patience with which one waits for a kettle to boil, as I walk restlessly up and down, seeking the most shallow looking place over which to cross. Eventually, by trial and error, I slide my wellingtons through mud and water until the level of the latter all but reaches their tops. At last I am over, and no further time is wasted as I slop across the muds in the direction of the saltings.

My programme is a simple one, for I am travelling light, with no food, no decoys, no impedimenta save a gun and fifty cartridges. I shall wait the turn of the tide, when the estuary begins to fill, hidden away in a shallow creek sheltered by rushes. On the muds and sand-banks about the mouth of the estuary and beyond, duck, curlew and the " smaller beer " are resting. When the tide turns and begins to wash upwards over these sanctuaries, the birds will be forced to rise.

From *The Gun on Saltings and Stubble*
by Noel M. Sedgwick, 1949.

GOIN' FISHIN'

EEL-BABBING is one of the simplest kinds of fishing. Tie a bit of wool on a line and offer it to the eel; if you are lucky he thinks it is a worm, takes a big bite at it, and gets the wool so tangled in his teeth that all you have to do is to pull him put.

From *The Last Stronghold of Sail*
by Hervey Benham, 1948.

VILLAGE CRICKET

IT is almost impossible to describe village cricket at its superb best. Those people who confuse it either with a game or a religion have given it a bad name in some quarters, but for those who enjoy its peculiar attributes there is no spectacle in the world to take its place. This kind of cricket is a country sport like fishing or making love. For those who do not know it well, perhaps I might venture to set down why I personally find it so good to watch.

Primarily, village cricket is a performance, and has something in common with the Lancers and much with the Harlequinade. It epitomizes the very English secret of combining individualism with co-operative effort. Each player has his chance to shine alone, and yet his final success or failure is the team's. Best of all, the day is never lost until it is won. At any moment a thumping miracle may happen, and usually does. In fact there is a lot of magic in it, and I do not use the word in any poetic sense. The whole business has something of the elements of a rustic charm, and on the right day, in the leafy privacy of the meadow and conducted by the right country people, a very potent sort of atmosphere indeed can be conjured up.

August Monday 1938 in Auburn (Tolleshunt D'Arcy) was one of these occasions.

From *The Oaken Heart*
by Margery Allingham, 1959.

MESSING ABOUT IN BOATS

THE Crouch is a splendid creek for sailing; there is 13ft. at low water where we are now, and we are just off where the coastguard vessel used to be, near East Neyland Clump, at Foulness. Abreast of Burnham there is 20ft. at low water, and we can sail right up to

Fambridge at the same time of tide. Another point about the Crouch is that it is a downright honest creek; there are no bars or banks to hurt anywhere until we get opposite Cricksea Ferry, a mile past Burnham, and that is buoyed with a rustic log of wood, which, however, answers all purposes.

The river averages from three-quarters-of-a-mile to a mile wide all the way up to Burnham, and so we have plenty of room to beat up . . .

We need not trouble ourselves about a berth, the river is broad and deep, and there is plenty of room. We choose a spot astern of a tidy-looking dredger. Get in the jib; down with the foresail. See how she shoots up! The main sheet is hauled in. The peak falls. All way is off her. " Yes! let go," and so for the third night the anchor holds us to the ground.

What a glorious sail we have had, and what a feed we mean to have! There is no mistake about that.

From *Sailing Tours, Part 1*
by Frank Cowper, 1892.

Section 12

FEASTS AND FESTIVALS

A FOREIGNER REMEMBERS

WE enjoyed the first English supper immensely. We were given slices of beef and veal, cut very thin and beaten tender, about the size of a hand, sprinkled with bread crumbs and grilled and nicely served on a silver dish; fine, big potatoes with salt butter to follow; delicious beer and a good Bordeaux wine.

Sophie in London
by Sophie La Roche.

From *Essex at Work, 1700-1815*
by A. F. J. Brown, 1969.

CHRISTMAS CHEER

GOOD husband and huswife, now chiefly be
glad,
things handsome to have, as they ought
to be had.
They both do provide, against Christmas do come,
to welcom their neighbors, good chere to have
some.
Good bread and good drinke, a good fier in the hall,
brawne, pudding, and souse, and good mustarde
withal.
Biefe, mutton, and Porke, and good Pies of the best,
pig, veale, goose, and capon, and turkey
wel drest,
Chese, apples and nuttes, and good Caroles to heare,
as then, in the cuntrey is counted good cheere.

What cost to good husbande, is any of this?
good housholde provision onely it is:
Of other the like, I do leave out a meny,
that costeth the husband never a peny.

From *Five Hundred Points of Husbandry*
by Thomas Tusser, 1571.

CHRISTMAS SUPPER AT THE " WHEATSHEAF "

WALTER announced the supper with becoming dignity.

" Come on now, gen'lemen, mates and neighbours, we're all here, so come and set down and make yerselves at home loike."

Soon the rich, warm smell of dismembered rabbit pie mingled with the contented munching of human jaws, a sound which is only comparable with that made by pigs, cows and other animals when engaged in precisely the same exercise. The rabbit pie was followed by a very good Christmas pudding, and the whole cemented with copious draughts of beer of a particularly excellent variety which makes the " Wheatsheaf " a thing apart among the pubs of the surrounding villages.

When the long table which had borne the feast was cleared away, chairs were drawn up to the fire, pipes were lit . . . and all settled down with that warm and comfortable, not to say peaceful feeling peculiar to the after effects of a good meal coupled with a good digestion. During this quiet lull the weather, rates, the parish council and swine fever were again the chief topics . . .

A rumble of laughter from the other side of the fireplace drew our attention to where the Warren brothers were trying to get Adam Saltmarsh to sing a song.

" Come on, Adam mate, sing us a good owd song, booy, we knows yer can, so doan't put ut off n'longer."

Under the influence of a frequently filled and equally quickly emptied mug, Adam was evidently giving way, while the company were getting increasingly vociferous in demanding a song.

At length Adam rose a little unsteadily to his feet . . . adjusted his mental capacities to sing . . . until, with a final dive into his beer mug, which he still clutched in one hand, Adam began his song . . .

At last " my trew luv " came to an end amid a thunder of applause and stampings. . .

The room was by this time getting uncomfortably hot and thick with tobacco smoke . . .

Reuben Deddens was becoming every minute more lively and was very anxious to tell a tale, but . . . No one paid much attention to his vociferous wails, and as young Harvey had tied his coat to the chair, the worthy sexton was fairly safe and too far gone to realize why he could not get up, so with a look of resignation, he reclined in the arms of Bacchus.

All were by this time getting in a rollicking mood and demanded choruses and songs to an extent that " John Peel " with " halloes " of thunderous power were inextricably mixed up with " Little Brown Jug," " Dolly Grey " and " A Bicycle Made for Two " . . .

" Now then, mates, now then," broke in the voice of John Mead. " Time's a gitten on, and us wants another good owd song afore us goos, so what shall ut be? Th'as Christmas time, so we ought to set about an owd car'l, I reckon," and without more ado he started on " I saw three ships come sailing in," a little quavery at first, but gathering strength and confidence as he proceeded, and as one by one some of the rough voices joined in with him . . .

As the old carol came to an end . . . someone started up the " Lincolnshire Poacher," which soon got mixed up with " Hearts of Oak " . . . Things were taking an uproarious turn, but as it was supposed to be a private party, Walter was feeling fairly safe from a visitation by the representative of law and order.

Time was getting on towards eleven, and some of the party had a good three miles to go, even if they went by the fields, whilst most had as much cargo as they could carry . . .

By ones and twos the party broke up, and found its way into the roadway. A young moon hung in a deep violet sky, and all was quiet and peace . . .

From *Essex Folk*
by Edward S. Knights, 1935.

CHRISTMAS DAY IN THE WORKHOUSE

THIS year the poor in the Union-houses of Chelmsford, Halstead, Maldon and Rochford received an extra allowance on Christmas Day. At Braintree the inmates of the house had roast beef and plum pudding, a pint of strong beer for each adult, half a pint to each child; pipes, tobacco and snuff were also given. Pretty doings at Braintree, truly! At Romford, to the disgrace of the Guardians, the paupers, 400 in number, had 240 plum puddings, weighing in all 600lbs. What an uproar these proceedings will make at Somerset House. Paupers eating plum-puddings on Christmas Day! What will this world come to?

From *The Essex Standard* 1841 included in
English History from Essex Sources
by A. C. Edwards, 1952.

THE YEARLY DISTRESS
OR, TITHING-TIME AT STOCK, IN ESSEX

Verses addressed to a country clergyman complaining of the disagreeableness of the day annually appointed for receiving the dues at the parsonage.

COME, ponder well, for 'tis no jest,
To laugh it would be wrong,
The troubles of a worthy priest,
The burthen of my song.

This priest he merry is and blithe
Three quarters of a year,
But oh! it cuts him like a scythe
When tithing-time draws near.

He then is full of frights and fears,
As one at point to die,
And long before the day appears
He heaves up many a sigh.

For then the farmers come, jog, jog,
  Along the miry road,
Each heart as heavy as a log,
  To make their payments good.

In sooth the sorrow of such days
  Is not to be express'd,
When he that takes and he that pays
  Are both alike distress'd.

. . . . .

The dinner comes, and down they sit:
  Were e'er such hungry folk?
There's little talking, and no wit;
  It is no time to joke.

One wipes his nose upon his sleeve,
  One spits upon the floor,
Yet not to give offence or grieve,
  Holds up the cloth before.

The punch goes round, and they are dull
  And lumpish still as ever;
Like barrels with their bellies full,
  They only weigh the heavier.

At length the busy time begins.
  " Come, neighbours, we must wag,"—
The money chinks, down drop their chins,
  Each lugging out his bag.

One talks of mildew and of frost,
  And one of storms of hail,
And one of pigs that he has lost
  By maggots at the tail.

Quoth one, " A rarer man than you
  In pulpit none shall hear;
But yet methinks to tell you true,
  You sell it plaguy dear."

Oh why were farmers made so coarse,
  Or clergy made so fine?
A kick that scarce would move a horse,
  May kill a sound divine.

From *The Poetical Works of Wm. Cooper* (1731-1800).

HARVEST SUPPER

ANOTHER old harvest custom was the harvest supper, consisting of roast beef, pudding and gravy, rabbit pie, apple pasties and plum pudding, with plenty of beer to wash it down; a repast which was given by the farmer to his harvesters at the end of the harvest. At the beginning of the feast, a verse something after the following was sung:

Here's a health to our master,
  The Lord of the feast,
God bless his endeavours,
  And send him increase;
May prosper his crop, boys,
  That we reap next year,
Here's a health to our master, boys,
  Drink up your beer.

From *Essex Folk*
by Edward S. Knights, 1935.

THE SUNDAY SCHOOL TREAT

THE Sunday school annual treat was for most village children " the " treat and the only one, unless there was a Christmas tea, in which case the two functions shared honours. On the morning of the great day, the tea tent was erected in one corner of the Rectory meadow, a lovely little field bordered on three sides by high hedges... In the tea tent were cut the thick slices of bread and butter and bread and cheese; large slabs of cake were cut up and buns put ready in baskets, and all prepared for the feast. In the early afternoon the children arrived and spent the time until the tea was ready in taking part in sports arranged by the Rector, in which the prizes were small bags of sweets. At half-past four came the tea, when all the children sat down under the shade of the two big chestnut trees, between which the tea tent was pitched. Never were such hungry children as those at Sunday school teas; bread and butter, buns and cake and many, many cups of tea went the same way among the laughing, happy throng. After the tea came more games and races while the helpers had their teas. About seven o'clock the party broke up with a little speech by the Rector, when each child went home happy and contented with a little bag of "hundreds and thousands," the annual gift of the wife of the Rector's warden, who was a notorious figure on treat day, as she came bearing her burden of "hundreds and thousands."

From *Essex Folk*
by Edward S. Knights, 1935.

A POACHER'S WEDDING

FATHER was strict as ever with the shooting of us boys.

'Let finger, brain and eye work together,' he would say . . .

I was with him shooting on the very morning of my wedding.

We had had early breakfast, for the wedding was to be at nine. And there we were, blazing away, with the church waiting quietly, just across the fields.

Father suddenly looked at his watch: put it back in his pocket. 'Boy,' he said, 'time you were across the road to be married. It's a serious job, getting married. Put that gun in the shed for now.'

We went across to the church together. And later, I went back with him, to the shooting, till dinner time.

After dinner, we were left alone, just my wife and I.

We sat by the fireside, and played records on an old Edison-Bell phonograph with cylindrical records, the only instrument we possessed. We were poor, but rich with the thoughts of our love, and of the years that lay ahead. How hard they were to be no one could guess. But their symbol stood in the corner of the little room, the firelight glinting in it—a new twelve-bore gun, my wife's wedding gift to me, and one for which she had been saving for many months from her earnings.

Wedding breakfast? Wedding cake? We had the wedding cake, a slab of plain shop cake, all we could afford. We could have been no happier with riches. We were secure in each other; we understood one another: I had married the daughter of a net-maker and poacher.

From *A Poacher's Tale*
as told by A. T. Curtis and related by Fred J. Speakman, 1961.

Section 13

PARSON'S PLEASURE

CHRISTIANS AWAKE!

IN these days when churches are coming closer together in understanding and association, there is a great need in every county for a central organisation which will collect, correlate and publish the record of achievements great and small by *all* churches. It is not enough for Christian effort to be achieved—it must be widely *seen* to be achieved.

From *History of Christianity in the Essex Region*
The Essex Education Committee, 1964.

CHRISTIANITY COMES TO ESSEX

The East Saxons are re-converted by the preaching of Cedd.

HAVING now become a citizen of the kingdom of heaven, Sigbert returned to his earthly capital after asking Oswy to send him teachers to convert his people to the Faith of Christ and baptize them. Accordingly the king sent to the province of the Middle Angles and summoned the man of God, Cedd, whom he despatched with another priest as companion to evangelise the East Saxons. And when these priests had visited the entire province and established a strong Christian community, Cedd returned home to Lindisfarne for consultations with Bishop Finan. When the latter learned the great success of his preaching, he invited two other bishops to assist him, and consecrated Cedd Bishop of the East Saxons. And when Cedd had been raised to the dignity of bi hop, he returned to his province and used his increased authority to promote the work already begun. He built churches in several places, and ordained priests and deacons to assist in teaching the

Faith and baptizing the people, especially in the city which the Saxons call *YTHANCESTIR* (Bradwell-on-Sea) and that called *TILEBURG* (Tilbury). The former place stands on the bank of the River Pante, the latter on the River Thames. Here Cedd established communities of the servants of Christ, and taught them to maintain the discipline of the regular life so far as these untutored folk were then capable of doing.

To the great joy of the King and all his people, the Gospel of eternal life made daily headway throughout the province . . .

From *A History of the English Church and People*
by the Venerable Bede
translated by Leo Sherley-Price, 1955.

HOLY GROUND

THE shrine of St. Edmund at Greensted . . . is literally a log-house. Its walls were formed of the forest trees, cleft in twain and set upright, the bottoms resting upon a cill, and the tops, rudely bevelled off, let into a groove at the top. The split portions of the trees placed side by side form a level surface within, and the rough and rounded parts are turned to the sun and storm without . . . Yet this primitive wall of unhewn planks has defied time and the worm for more than eight centuries. This was the shrine in which the body of St. Edmund rested in 1013 on its way to its final burial place at Bury . . . While gazing upon the curious and venerable edifice, the mind is carried back to the scene of the cowled band halting in the bush, no habitable resting-place within reach, and depositing the body of the sainted king beneath the shelter reared from the spoil of the surrounding forest, their torches glimmering through the brushwood, and the solemn chant of the watchers through the night breaking upon the ear. To the Saxon mind the ground became holy . . . In the days of masses and miracles it was no doubt a place of frequent resort; and even now the church is an object well worthy to tempt the foot of the antiquarian pilgrim.

From *The People's History of Essex*
by D. W. Coller, 1861.

A REG'LAR BAD 'UN

THE old man chuckled to himself . . . while he looked out across the bright sunlit fields, with eyes which evidently saw more of the past than the brilliance and glory of the present.

Suddenly turning towards me, William said: "There's a many owd uns buried in this here place what I've knowed in me young days, and some on 'em weren't no better'n they ort to a bin, be no means," he added, with the authority of one who by the indisputable fact of being still in the flesh was thus privileged to refer to those who had gone before.

"You see that 'ere grave over there," he said with a flourish of his broom in the direction of a somewhat decrepit wooden cross which was being supported in the fragrant arms of a lavender bush. "Owd 'lijah Bugg's in that 'ere, 'cos I helped to put 'um there, so I know. He were parish clerk of Orsett St. Giles (our neighbouring village), a reg'lar bad 'un he were, so bad as his pore wife had him buried here to be well out of her way. He used to treat she crule, he did . . ."

From *Essex Folk*
by Edward S. Knights, 1935.

THE RUSTIC SUNDAY

LET me recommend as an agreeable sensation a six-mile country walk to Church on a fine Sunday. If your mind, gentle reader, has yet some "dregs of virtue" left in it, you will find it satisfying, believe me, to feel that for once you are not in bed at 8.30 o'clock on Sunday morning, that you have had your breakfast, that you are enjoying the splendid sunshine and the fresh morning air before it has had time to get heated and tiring, and that, having "shaken off dull sloth," you are on your way, like a decent member of the community, to Church. Without gloves, too, without a high and heavy hat, with an ordinary loose light suit, and no prayer-book to carry, and with a pipe or cigar if you like in your mouth for companionship and comfort.

Somewhat thus I set forth from the cleanly, comfortable, well-appointed old George Hotel at Halstead, one Sunday morning in spring. By the time I had walked half a mile, I was so overcome by the feeling of virtue and the influences of nature, the perfect repose and quiet of the country, the songs of the birds, and the sound of the Halstead Church bells growing more and more distant, the wonderful verdure of the sunlit landscape, the tranquil enjoyment of certain Sabbath-keeping cart-horses, that I was in a delicious state of reverie and felt the inspiration of poetic composition coming strongly upon me . . .

I walked on past quiet cottages and through a small village or two, where the fathers and mothers were respectively interesting themselves in their gardens and children, and at last I came to a small quaint old church, which seemed to me to be the place to see the rustic churchgoer to advantage. So I inspected the Churchyard and stretched myself on the grass to wait for Church time. At 10.15 the bell began; soon the Clergyman came up, and at twenty-five minutes past ten I followed him in. He soon emerged from the vestry to see what congregation he had. He looked pleased when he saw me, and appeared after a few more minutes' interval, to see if anyone else had arrived. As no one had come, he again disappeared. I enquired of the bell-ringer when the service began. He said at half-past ten. After two minutes' anxious pause, *I hurriedly fled*, having no fancy to go through a service with only the Clergyman and Clerk for company. I made my way with all speed along the high-road, until I came to another and larger Church, where the people were assembling in good numbers, and where the service began at eleven o'clock. An *excellently conducted* service it was. Attractive and earnest, with a surpliced Choir and a good congregation, and an admirable sermon, couched in the simplest language, which might well be " understanded " even of the simple people there assembled . . .

All the seats were free, with the exception of the family chapel of the squire—who came in late, according to a fashion which seems to have prevailed for nearly three centuries at least . . .

It was a wonderful choir . . . There was scarcely any perceptible dialect or twang, and they sang to the accompaniment of a harmonium with vigour and correctness. As for the congregation, it was a fairly attentive one, and quite representative of all classes in the parish . . .

After Church I walked through the parish and made for the next. As I passed the beer-house and inn I saw no signs of Sunday drinking on the part of the labourers. Everything seemed quiet and orderly and contented.

From *The Essex Labourer*
by W. Gurney Benham, 1888.

GLORY BE!

LOOK at that Council meetin' here las' week—
Why bless my saoul if Tom din taike the chair,
An' Parson settin' 'gin the door as meek
As some owd sheep, I tell yer; that he were.

An' what d'yer think they done? wh' nought, o' course,
Cos there aint nothin' here want doin' to.
N' wonner Parson he look drefful cross
Comin' awäy; I see him, didn't you?

An' I don't howd 'ith these 'ere wäys at Charch—
A singin' o' the Scripters an' that 'ere,
Dressin' theirselves in nightgownds stiff wi' starch:
The Boible never tell 'em that, I swear.

They säy *Ah*men instead o' *Ai*men now;
Tha's only jes to be contrairy like,
An' when that come the 'Glory be' thäy bow
An' cartsey. Lor, I'd like to gim a shaike.

D'yer think the Aingels sing *Ah*men? Not thäy,
An' when these 'ere are dead an' gone th'll see,
Th'll give it to 'em sträight up there, th'll säy
'You ent a go'n to sing along o' we.'

I ent owd-fashioned, nao, I loike to see
The young uns comin' on. But now-a-däys
They säy an' do sich things git over me,
An' I carnt howd 'ith these new-fangled wäys.

From *Essex Ballads*
by Charles Edwin Benham, 1895.

PARSON WARING . . . ECCENTRIC EXTRAORDINARY

PARSON Waring assuredly excelled all competitors for the fame of eccentricity. No single action of his life, as far as could be known, in which it was possible for him to deviate from the rest of mankind, did he perform in accordance with general usage. He was instituted to the Vicarage of Heybridge in 1798 and . . . also the curacies of S. Mary, Maldon, and of Mundon . . . He was also Librarian to Dr. Plume's Library at Maldon, and . . . also Master of the Grammar School founded by the same person . . .

In stature he was about the middle height, or a little below it, stoutly built and a little inclined to corpulence. His hair was dark, parted on one side, and brushed off the forehead, and he wore whiskers . . . His lower lip was rather protuberant and curved. His attire (was) of the most singular kind. His usual dress was a light blue-grey coat called "pepper and salt," something between a shooting jacket and surtout, cut straight and reaching a few inches below the hips. This was buttoned top and bottom and a coloured silk handkerchief was thrust in the breast. His nether garment was black and of the same hybrid description as the coat for it was neither pantaloon nor breeches . . . Light stockings and low shoes, and most commonly white linen gaiters very loose, a coloured silk handkerchief (generally yellow with white spots) twisted loosely round his neck, and a rather shabby low crowned hat completed his singular and unclerical costume . . .

He was a remarkably temperate man . . . I once met him at a musical party and remember that he only drank a little ale. He was a great proficient in music and played admirably upon the violoncello and . . . on other instruments also. He was a great wit and his conversation was brilliant and facetious . . . He was even amusing upon the subject of his own eccentricities . . .

It is to be regretted that Mr. Waring gave full scope to his eccentricities in the church and was extremely negligent, loose and irregular in the performance of Divine Service. I do not believe that this arose from irreverence but unfortunately he lived in a time of great laxity in church discipline . . . Once in the desk, the whole service was a regular scamper. He was naturally a fine reader but went through the service with astonishing rapidity, waiting neither for clerk nor congregation in their verses or responses . . . His sermons rarely extended beyond fifteen minutes. Sometimes they lasted only ten . . . Before his discourse he always repeated the second collect for Advent omitting the word "learn." More than once I have seen him lean over the pulpit and read his text from the large Bible in the desk beneath. Latterly psalmody was introduced into St. Mary's, and bad enough it was. As I have said Mr. Waring was an accomplished musician, and I hardly know whether he objected more to the discordance of the choir than to their lengthening the service. Be that as it may he seemed to have a strong aversion to their music and there was sometimes an earnest struggle whether he should pronounce the Blessing ere they should give out their final hymn . . .

I might add many other instances of Parson Waring's eccentricity . . . in short he did nothing like his fellow creatures. He enjoyed the reputation of being a great scholar and a great wit but I never heard that he made any beneficial use of his learning . . . He was a man of high moral character, and integrity. Benevolent, affable, courteous. Greatly respected by all persons, I doubt if he had an enemy even among those who most condemned his conduct as a clergyman. Eccentricity is not proof of aberration of intellect; and I am not without suspicion that the origin of Mr. Waring's eccentricity may have been his limited income.

He cared not for display, cared less for the opinion of the world and having commenced a certain course carried it out consistently. . . . His peculiarities came forth spontaneously, seemed perfectly natural to him and unstudied. No one expected to see him act as other men; he never forgot himself but sustained his character to the last.

From *Ecclesiae Essexienses*
by H. W. King.

"*THE PREACHING WILL GO ON*"

CONRAD NOEL is famous as a pioneer of Christian Socialism and or his unique treatment of Thaxted Church and its Services. He was born in 1869 of a progressive aristocratic family and took Holy Orders in the Church of England in 1894. He was a disciple of Frederick Dennison Maurice the Christian socialist theologian and philosopher and was a member of Father Stewart Headlam's Guild of St. Matthew. Later he became organising secretary of the Church Socialist League for which he spoke all over the country...

Unlike so many of the progressive clergy his politics and religion were not in separate compartments; rather his politics and socialism flowed out of his theology.

He was an intense anti-imperialist and was for many years chairman of the Anti-Imperialist League. For this reason he supported the movements for the freedom of Ireland and India, a stand which brought him much opposition. He too was no pacifist. He supported the cause of the allies in both world wars. In 1914 he had the flags of the allies in church and along with them the red flag of the International and on it the words " He hath made of one blood all nations." It was during the miners strike of 1921 that someone objected to the red flag and removed it. Conrad replaced it. It was pulled down again by students from Cambridge. He put up another higher in the church and had it guarded night and day. But later a Church Consistory Court ordered its removal. He then said defiantly from the pulpit " That flag has been removed but the preaching will go on"...

He readily supported the workers in all their struggles for better conditions ...

Needless to say his courageous stand brought him many friends and admirers, among whom was the great Archbishop Temple. But he also encountered very bitter opposition and hostility, and this was the measure of his courage and conviction that he never wavered . . .

By nature he was the kindliest of men, with his brown eyes and curly hair and determined chin; with a rare wit and humour. He had great personal charm and the gift of drawing everyone into his own immediate interests and enthusiasms . . .

His whole life was a living challenge of justice on behalf of the oppressed peoples and nations of the world.

He was laid to rest in the churchyard near to the High Altar of the church he had loved and served so well, and on his tombstone are the words:

" He loved justice and hated oppression."

From *Men of Vision*—a broadcast talk given
by Jack Putterill, 1962.

Section 14

CURES AND REMEDIES

" He who cures a disease may be the skilfulest,
but he that prevents it is the safest physician."

From *Worthies of England*
by Thomas Fuller, 1608-1661.

PREVENTION IS BETTER THAN CURE

IN 1640 a number of the inhabitants of Rayleigh complained to the Justices concerning one of the townspeople having a case of small-pox in his house. Their suggested " remedy " applies to things other than small-pox it would seem.

To the right honourable and worshipfull his Majesties Justices of the Peace for this County the Humble Petition of the Inhabitantes of Rayleigh.

Most humbly shew unto your Honours and Worships the Inhabitantes of Rayleigh . . . that Thomas Read of our said parish Victualler & Butcher is a disordered person given to drincking & quarrelling and does frequently suffer poore labouring Townsemen to sitt tipling and drincking in his house to the undoeing of their families and more especially the said Read upon the first day of June last past being our Fair day having a child newly dead of the smale Pox and knowing his house to be infected did conceale the same entertaining a multitude of guests whereby many were infected one of our own Town is dead, many other in severall places sicke, and the contagion carryed to other places wherefore our humble Petition is that your Honours and Worships wilbe pleased to suppress the said Read from Keeping of victualling in his house (wee having too many Victuallers in the Town besides) and wee shall pray for your honours and worships health and prosperity long to continue.

From *Quarter Sessions Records—The Essex Record Office.*

A SWEET AND PLEASANT, WHOLESOME AND MEDICINAL HERB

THERE were two maids talking of husbands, which is for the most part the theme of their discourse, and the subject of their thoughts.

The one said: " I would not marry a man that takes tobacco, for anything."

" Then," said the other, " it is likely you will have a fool for your husband; for tobacco is able to make a fool a wise man: and though it doth not always work wise effects, by reason some fools are beyond all improvement, yet it never fails where any improvement is to be made."

" Why," said the first, " what wise effects does it work? "

The second said: " It composes the mind, it busies the thoughts, represents several objects to the mind's view, settles and stays the senses, clears the understanding, strengthens the judgement, spies out errors, evaporates follies, heals ambition, comforts sorrow, abates passions, excites to noble action, digests conception, enlarges knowledge, elevates imaginations, creates fancies, quickens wit, and makes reason pleader and truth judge in all disputes or controversies betwixt right and wrong."

The first said: " It makes the breath stink."

" You mistake," said the second, " it will make a stinking breath sweet."

" It is a beastly smell," said the first.

Said the second: " Civet is a beastly smell, and that you will thrust your nose to, although it be an excrement; and for anything we know, so is ambergris; then tobacco is a sweet and pleasant, wholesome and medicinal herb."

From *Feigned Stories in Prose*
Margaret Cavendish, Duchess of Newcastle, 1656.

THINGS GOOD FOR THE HEART

SAFFRON, Borage, Harts horn, Mustard, Cloves, Galingale, Nutmegs, Red Roses, Violets, Mace, Sugar, good Wine moderately taken, Mirth and good air . . .

FOR THE YELLOW JAUNDICE

TAKE Elecampane roots, and the inner bark of the Barbery, of each six ounces; of Salendine roots eight ounces; of English Saffron the weight of a groat: seethe all these in a pinte of White-wine, strain it, and drink thereof four spoonfulls morning and evening warm . . .

FOR CONVULSION FITS

TAKE white Coperas (found off Harwich) and dissolve it in a little warm distilled water, and then with cleane lists laid into it filter it from the drosse, and gently vapour away the water till it be dry; then dis olve it again, filter it, and lay it again in an oven as before, and it is prepared: Hereof you may give unto a sucking child three grains in a spoonful of posset-drink once or twice, and it seldome or never faileth, but cureth.

From *The Most Choice Receipts of Physick and Chyrurgery*
by Ralph Williams, 1652.

AN INFALLIBLE CURE FOR AN AGUE

OF the best Jesuits' Bark, half an ounce, powdered; salt of wormwood, forty grains; snake root, powdered, forty grains; one nutmeg, grated.

Mix the powders together and divide it in 6 or 8 papers. Take one every two or three hours in a glass of red wine. You must begin to take it as soon as the fit goes off, and it must all be taken before the time you expect the next fit . . .

From *English History from Essex Sources*
by A. C. Edwards

MRS. COPE'S ESSENCE OF VIPERS

TAKE a live viper, cut off the head, take out the guts and fat and strip off the skin, all which must be thrown away. Then take the viper and put it into a pint bottle, to a quarter of a pint of water; cork up the bottle and tie it down. Then put the bottle in a kettle of water, and boil it an hour. When the heat is something abated, strain it through muslin and drink the whole at once, going to bed or in a morning, fasting. The bottle must be put into the kettle of water whilst cold. You may continue this as long as you find occasion, for it is a great restorative.

From *English History from Essex Sources*
by A. C. Edwards, 1952.

THE SNAIL GRUEL FOR A CONSUMPTION

TAKE 40 garden snails, pick off the shells, then boil 'em in a quart of spring water with a spoonful of pearl barley and a spoonful of hartshorn shavings till it's wasted to a pint. Then strain it, add to it half a pint of milk, sweeten it to your taste with eringo roots [sea-holly found around the coast and once processed by a family in the Colchester district], let the person drink half a pint of this first in a morning and last at night going to bed, if their stomach can bear as much. Every other day is often enough to make it. It's very good for the rickets.

From *English History from Essex Sources*
by A. C. Edwards, 1952.

DOCTOR'S ORDERS—circa 1777

An extract from the Stansted Mountfitchet Overseers' Accounts.

				s. d.
March	19	A Corroborating mixture	Emd. Dench's child	1. 6
		A regrigerating lotion	....	1. 0
		Two purging powders	Rd. Phillips	1. 0
	20	A balsamic mixture	Gillbey's daughter..	2. 0
	24	A cathartic electuary	Rd. Markwell	2. 0
		Antirheumatic drops	Rd. Wright's wife ..	1. 0

April	21	Bleeding	Rd. Turner	0. 6
May	18	Bleeding at home	H. Griggs	1. 0
	24	A nervous mixture	....	2. 0
July	17	A cephallic mixture	Plumb's wife	1. 0
	28	Drawing a tooth	Mary Saville	0. 6

From *The Essex Record Office.*

DR. DAFFY'S ELIXIR

An advertisement in the Ipswich Journal *for March 17, 1749, stated that Dr. Thomas Daffy's elixir could be purchased from J. Pilborough, a printer in Colchester . . . The advertisement pronounced that Dr. Daffy's cordial drink was:*

" UNIVERSALLY allowed to be the most beneficial Cordial in the World and a Sovereign Remedy in most Distempers incident to Mankind. 'Tis no trifling thing to allure the Publick withal, but a real and well experienced medicine . . . approved of and recommended by several of the most eminent of the College of Physicians in London who declared it the best medicine ever exposed to Sale. For more than 80 years past this Nobel Elixir hath had wonderful success in curing and relieving Persons of all Ages afflicted with the Cholick, Ghout, Rheumatism, Stone and Gravel, Worms, Scurvy, Dropsy, Black and Yellow Jaundice, Surfeits, Gripes or Piles. And in all other Distempers where purging is required this Cordial assists Nature in the most agreeable manner, as appears by the number of cures it has performed."

From *Essex Countryside*
by Maurice Lindsay, 1968.

A CURE FOR WHOOPING COUGH

TAN Scanner's van hove in sight laden with pots and pans and mats of various vivid colours . . .

" Yer mother in, Missie? " he enquired affably.

" Round at the back," said Tilda, and gave another cough . . .

" Dear me," said Scanner. " God a bad cough, ain't yer, Missie?"

" That I have," said Tilda. " Proper 'hooping that is."

" 'Ooping," said Scanner. " Well, I never. If yer was mine I'd set that ter rights and quick."

" Would yer? "

" Ah, that I would. Tell yer mother what to do I will and that'll goo in a flash, see ef it don't."

" No that 'ont," said Tilda. " Keep me here for a month n'more so they say. I'm going ter see the doctor in the 'spensary this morning. He'll know."

. . . Scanner passed round to the back door with the assortment of pans and gaudy coloured mats . . .

" Dear me . . . ef that little gal o' yourn ain't bin and got the 'ooping," and he clicked his tongue sympathetically.

" Not proper she ain't yet," said her mother. " She only started ter cough this morning. We're taking her ter the doctor to-day so he'll tell if she's got ut."

" Ah, they don't know everything, them doctors," said Scanner. " I could tell 'em a lot as they don't, that I could. Now I'll just tell ye what to do with that little gal o' yourn, missis, and that'll just put 'er all to rights and quick that will. Fust yer draw 'er back'ards through a quick bush and then you get a meece, a nice young meece . . . "

" A what? " said Tilda's mother.

" A meece," said Scanner—he hesitated—" A moose I mean."

" Yer mean a mouse," said Tilda's mother.

" Yes, a mouse you call it. Well, yer get a nice young meece and bake it in its jacket and make 'er swaller it 'ole. That'll do it, see if it don't. She 'ont never cough agin. Certain cure that is, I'll promise yer that is."

Tilda's mouth opened wide. She had a horror of mice, dead or alive . . .

" Never be troubled agin," said Scanner with emphasis, " you'll see she 'ont and you'll thank me for telling yer, that yer will, and now Missis, if yer want any nice little mats or good little kettles I've got a lot 'ere that's a bargain ter anybody . . . "

But Tilda's mother wasn't wanting any mats at one-and-nine or kettles at ninepence. Something else in Scanner's miscellaneous collection of oddments attracted her attention.

" You've got a mouse trap there," she said. " I'll have that."
Tilda at the doorway gave a shudder.
" That's right, Missis, good little trap that is . . . "

From *The Magic Mawkin & Other Essex Tales*
by H. Cranmer-Byng.

A CERTAIN CURE FOR EAR-ACHE

I HAVE lately heard of a country cure for ear trouble. Apparently years ago the daughter of a friend of mine living in Margaretting had discharging ears, and was advised by a gipsy to skim the fat from the water in which a hedgehog had been boiled and put a teaspoonful of it warmed in the child's ears. This they did, and the trouble quickly cleared up and never returned.

From *Essex Countryside*,
by Margaret Ricketts, 1970.

THE IDEAL EXERCISE

. . . WALKING is the normal means of progression. Nature has given it her blessing. Demanding an upright carriage, filling the lungs with pure air, and bringing all the muscles of the body into play, it is the ideal exercise, and the best physic I know. For the cure of any of the nervous ills of modern life, give me twenty-four hours with my feet on the gravel or the grass. Essex is a pedestrian's paradise.

From *Romantic Essex*
by Reginald A. Beckett, 1901.

Section 15

LORE AND LEGEND

END OF A FIERY MONSTER

WHAT other district in the whole of England has been favoured by a visit from a dragon?

This is not romance. It happened in 1405. John of Trokelowe and Henry of Blandforde have left an account . . . in monkish Latin which ranks as a first class piece of reporting. Recently, they say, at the village of Bures near Sudbury a dragon appeared, " vast in body, with a tufted head, saw-like teeth and a tail immeasurably long," which did evil by going to and fro among the sheep, killing many. At which the bowmen of Richard de Waldegrave, knight, on whose land the dragon lurked, moved out; but the body of the dragon turned the arrows aside, and they sprang back from its armour as if from stone or iron; and those arrows which fell on the spine of its back glanced off again and sprang away with clangings, as if they had struck plates of bronze. Whereupon the whole countryside was roused. But when the dragon saw the bowmen were advancing again to the attack it took refuge in the mere and hid among the reeds; nor was it any more seen.

From *Essex Pie*
by T. M. Hope, 1951.

MATTHEW HOPKINS—WITCHFINDER GENERAL

THE reign of James I was distinguished by great superstitions . . . Questions of sorcery and demonology were freely discussed, but all this was done academically. A stringent law, which almost imposed the necessity of believing in witchcraft, was passed in the early part of this reign. But this was really aloof—the popular mind was unaffected by excitement over the topic. It required an outside agency and the accumulation of other superstitions to awaken anything like persecution. Come it did, however, when Puritanism had become general; and, among the sectarian feeling which poured over the land toward the middle of the seventeenth century, there came a horrid mania for murdering people under the pretence of witchcraft.

It was in 1645 that this began. One Matthew Hopkins, son of a Suffolk minister, was settled at Manningtree. Supposed to have gained a living as a lawyer, he professed to have become acquainted with women at Manningtree who were witches. " Every six weeks they met on a Friday night and offered sacrifices to the Devil." After obtaining the condemnation of these poor women he set up as witchfinder general, " a trade never hitherto taken up in England . . . " The sort of stuff that imposed upon Christian society at this period may be best shown by the " examination " of one of the culprits, Elizabeth Clarke, an old woman, of Manningtree. The plan of Hopkins in dealing with a reputed witch was to prevent her sleeping until she made confession. In Clarke's case he watched with her several nights in the house of a Mr. Edwards, where she was detained, and was not permitted to sleep. After three nights of watching she broke silence and " confessed " that about six or seven years ago she had surrendered herself to the Devil, who came to her in the form of " a proper gentleman with a laced band." Soon after this a little dog appeared, fat and short in the legs, in colour white with sandy spots, which, when she hindered it from approaching her, vanished from sight. She confessed that it was one of her imps, named " Jarmara." Immediately after this had disappeared, another came in the form of a greyhound, which she called " Vinegar Tom," and it was followed by another in the shape of a polecat . . .

The career of this wretch Hopkins is one of the most monstrous things in our social history. After his success at Chelmsford Assizes he went about through Suffolk, Norfolk and Huntingdonshire. The poor, the old and the ignorant were easy victims to his avarice—for avarice it was. It was a lucky stroke of money-making, and he was well paid while the craze lasted: "Twenty shillings a head for every witch discovered." Hopkins posed as a great judge of Special Marks, and the load of guilt to be attached to them. But as a true criterion of the real witch, he adhered to the traditional mode of discovery—swim or sink. He would tie together the thumbs and toes of the suspected person, and give her a dowsing in a pond. Coming alive out of the water was deemed a certain proof of guilt. Sometimes the accused were tied neck and heels and tossed into a pond; if they floated they were guilty, and forthwith taken out and burnt or hanged; if they were innocent, they were " only drowned." In the end it was long believed that the experiment was tried on Hopkins himself, and coming out alive from the water he was condemned and executed as a wizard . . .

When Hopkins collapsed the great persecution was soon over.

From *Memorials of Old Essex*
Ed. A. Clifton Kelway, 1908.

AN INSTRUMENT OF STRANGE PURPORT

Of the relics of Cunning Murrell, the wise man of Essex, I have seen many, and I own some—his books of conjuration and geomancy, scores of his written horoscopes; and of his actual implements of magic I have seen the famous glass by which he, or anybody else, was enabled to see through a brick wall . . . it was by this and other such aids that Murrell became, and remained to his life's end, something like absolute sovereign of all Essex outside the great houses.

But there was another instrument of far stranger purport. There was talk of it still, twenty years and more after its reputed possessor was gathered to his fathers and his twenty-one children in Hadleigh Churchyard. This was said to be nothing less than a strange disc of dull copper, by aid whereof Cunning Murrell could distinguish the true man from a liar. For the liar might stare at it till his eyes were sore, yet never could he see in it anything but its mere material self—a round plate of common dull copper; while it was the peculiar virtue of an honest man's eyes to perceive on the dim surface *something*—something of which only Cunning Murrell had the secret; something which the gazer must declare to him as proof and test of his truth. But of what that something was nobody could tell a word; for indeed it would seem that nobody had ever seen it. And yet belief in its existence was as wide as Essex.

From *Cunning Murrell*
by Arthur Morrison.

OF GHOULIES AND GHOSTIES . . .

ALL these years . . . I have been in Borley, the story of the Rectory . . . has been part of my life . . .

I have a vivid recollection of one particular evening in July 1937. Mrs. Henning and I returned with him (Mr. Kerr-Pearse) to Borley.

As I went in, I carefully put the chain up at the front door, and I want to make it quite clear that we took every precaution to prevent anyone playing tricks on us. All the doors and windows were locked and sealed. The only entrance was the french window of the small study where we sat talking at a table. Insofar as it was humanly possible, we had made sure that there was no way in or out of the rectory except by that window.

There is little doubt, I fancy, that at such times when one is keyed up to a pitch, the slightest noise makes an impression. And the odd thing about the rectory, a fact I had noticed repeatedly since my first day inside it, was the abnormal quiet of the place. One had the idea that the vast block of masonry somehow protected you from the outside sounds and acted as proof against them. In a short time, the creaking of boards shrinking after dark in the cool of the night no longer disturbed you but, on a night such as this, I believe anyone who had sat with us would have been more than usually aware of anything out of the ordinary.

It was getting dusk. Mr. Kerr-Pearse was, if I remember, telling us of a conversation he had had with one of the villagers that morning, when there was a noise of someone opening a door. We sat and waited in silence and I can remember myself thinking how bright the light of the lamp was and that it needed turning down before it began to flare. I suppose subconsciously I was very glad to have that lamp there. If my eyes were fixed upon it, my ears and those of my companions were on the passage outside and the door which had opened. All of us had heard it. As for me, a curious pricking sensation came over me . . .

And then in the utter quiet of the night, we could hear footsteps coming up the long stone-flagged passage leading from the kitchen quarters and with the steps and, as it were, following after them, came a swishing noise as of long trailing garments. We rose slowly from our seats and still continued, in the frightening silence penetrated only by those footsteps, to wait. The whole house, the difference in our personalities, the very idea that we were impartial investigators who were supposed to be above being swept away by any emotion of any kind, were absorbed and concentrated into those footsteps where no footsteps should be, that opening door and swishing garments in a house we knew to be empty . . . They came down the long passage nearer and nearer to the study. Our bodies were tensed as if to ward off a blow and I had become, suddenly, thirsty.

When we could stand the tension no longer, we went to the door and opened it . . . Without a word, we ran into the passage and looked about us to see—nothing. The moment the door opened, the sounds ceased and the two nightlights, which had been placed in the passage, were still burning brightly.

From *Haunted Borley*
by A. C. Henning, 1948.

COGGESHALL JOBS

In the county of Essex, when anybody either does or proposes to do anything more than ordinarily foolish, it is customary to speak of it as a "Coggeshall job." The origin of the term has never been ascertained, but the "jobs," real or fictitious, which have been handed down strongly resemble the tales told of the Wiltshire "Moonrakers." Certainly of Coggeshall natives some curious stories are related at the present day; two of the most modern may be cited as examples. A man was told by his master to transplant an apple-tree. He cut the tree down first, and then dug up and carefully replanted the roots. To prevent people from being run over by railway trains a native proposed that the engines should always be fenced in, for then, as he expressed it, " the public will be safe on the other side."

From *Essex: Highways, Byways and Waterways*
by C. R. B. Barrett, 1892.

BEGETTING A WIFE

I SET out on the 3rd of *April*, 1722, going first Eastward . . . down by the coast of the *Thames* thro' the Marshes or Hundreds, on the South-side of the County of *Essex* . . .

This side of the County is rather rich in Land, than in Inhabitants, occasioned chiefly by the unhealthiness of the Air for these low Marsh Grounds . . . have been saved out of the River *Thames*, and out of the *Sea*.

. . . One Remark more, before I leave this damp part of the World, and which I cannot omit on the Women's Account; namely, that I took notice of a strange Decay of the Sex here; insomuch, that all along this Country it was very frequent to meet with Men that had had from five or six, to fourteen or fifteen Wives; nay, and some more; and I was inform'd that in the Marshes on the other Side of the River over-against *Candy* Island [Canvey Island], there was a Farmer, who was then living with the five and Twentieth Wife, and that his Son who was about 35 Years old, had already had about fourteen; indeed this part of the Story, I only had by Report, tho' from good Hands too; The reason, as a merry Fellow told me, who said he had had about a Dozen and a half of Wives, (tho' I found afterwards he Fibb'd a little) was this; That they being bred in the Marshes themselves, and season'd to the Place, did pretty well with it; but that they always went up into the Hilly Country, or to speak their own Language into the Uplands for a Wife: That when they took the young Lasses out of the wholesome and fresh Air, they were healthy, fresh, and clear, and well; but when they came out of their native Air into the Marshes among the Fogs and Damps, there they presently chang'd their Complexion, got an Ague or two, and seldom held it above half a Year, or a Year at most; and then, *said he*, we go to the Uplands again, and fetch another; so that marrying of Wives was reckon'd a kind of good Farm to them: It is true, the Fellow told this in a kind of Drollery, and Mirth; but the Fact, for all that, is certainly true; and that they have abundance of Wives by that very means.

From *A Tour Thro' the whole Island of Great Britain*
by Daniel Defoe, 1722.

LOVE WILL FIND A WAY

IN the days of good Queen Bess, there lived in that grey old Manor House, at Rochford, where the virgin Queen's fair mother had spent so many of her happy days, a girl of high degree, the Lady Frances Rich. She came of a great family, high in favour with the Tudor House. Many a time she must have thought of the fair girls who had lived there fifty years before, of the gay sister who so lightly pleased a king, and married twice to please herself; of that other long-haired, high-spirited merry girl, whose enticing resistance won a crown, w th death beneath.

Frances was just such a merry girl, but with her to love was to yield, and to yield was to dare. Among the gentlemen of the county who visited at her father's splendid palace of Leez or Leighs, was a Master John Cammock. In hunting, hawking, and the accomplishments of the time, Master Cammock ruffled it with the bravest. He and the Lady Frances were somehow always together, and so it happened before they either knew, their eyes met, and they found they were in love. But a squire of low degree, although a gentleman of coat-armour, like Master Cammock, could never hope to obtain the assent of the powerful Lord Rich, the wealthiest man in Essex, who had lately bought the ancestral home of the great Queen's mother. And so they loved, and lived on such stray chances as the rural life of a great family offered.

But finding their impatience could no longer be delayed, or else by the sudden promptings of the moment, it happened as the Lord Rich was moving his household from Leighs to Rochford, that the lovers, who had lagged beh nd to fly a hawk perhaps at a heron as it heavily rose from the marshes, seeing the long cavalcade disappearing up the narrow lane that led to Hockley, looked into each others eyes.

" Will you? " said Master Cammock.

" Aye, marry will I! " said Frances, with such a glance as sets men acting.

In another minute their horses' heads were turned towards the Crouch, and they were galloping hard down the lane for the ferry at Fambridge.

But there was a part of the cavalcade which had not quite disappeared. The rapid pace of the fugitives aroused suspicion. Lord Rich is warned, and a party start in pursuit, headed by Lord Rich himself.

" Aha! the ferry is at the other side, the boat is high and dry; they can't get over," laughed Lord Rich, but his laugh was not a merry one. Evidently it would go hard with Master Cammock if he were caught.

" They'll never dare it! " cried the peer.

But they will . . . The lady's horse could never swim that stream, it was dead beat already.

In haste Master Cammock undoes his belt. Lightly he lifts the girl out of her saddle and sits her before him, fastening the belt round both. Her arms are clasped round her lover; her bonnie face is close to his—bright eyes of trust and love.

" Now for life and love! Get in, my Bevis."

With cautious stride the powerful horse steps over the shingle and plunges into the water. The tide is running strong. It is nearly half a mile across.

" They'll never do it! " cries Lord Rich, as they rein up on the edge of the marsh aghast. " 'Twere well nigh death for one to do it; for two, and on a jaded beast, 'tis Kingdom come for sure," so moaned the father, and gazed with straining eyes.

The wind blew strong; the white-maned waves frothed against the little speck where three lives struggled to the shore.

Suddenly a loud whinny broke from Lord Rich's mare.

" Aye, aye! the jade. She wants stout Bevis back again. But, by my faith, she has not cried in vain, they're turning round!"

For a moment it seemed as if the cry had had effect. The black speck wavered. There was an instant of suspense.

"They'll drown before our eyes!" There was agony in the proud peer's voice. "I'd rather see her wed than drown like that. Well done; well sped, brave heart, they've won the farther shore. Ah! they're gone. Nay, 'twas a parlous, great wave. They're touching land. Thank God!"

And so indeed they did. The stout horse struggled to the bank. A moment they paused on the top, then cantered off, and so were lost in North Fambridge woods.

At Maldon that night was a hurried wedding, and Mistress Frances Rich became Dame Cammock before the day was done.

When the news reached Lord Rich, thankful at the escape of his daughter and accepting the inevitable, all he said was:

"She has even hazarded her life for him. God bless 'em!"

And this pious wish seems to have been fulfilled, in one sense at least. They had thirteen children—two sons and eleven daughters—whose effigies may be seen to this day in Maldon church, kneeling devoutly, two and two, save one, beneath their mother.

From *Sailing Tours Part 1*
by Frank Cowper, 1892.

THE DUNMOW FLITCH

AMONGST the very many curious customs or tenures found in various parts of the country dating from an early period, the "Dunmow Flitch" is unique and world-renowned. "By whom, or at what period, this custom was instituted is not certain, but it is generally ascribed to one of the family of Fitz-Walter. The bacon, generally a flitch (sometimes a gammon was given instead), could be claimed by any couple who had been married a year and a day . . . The couple desiring it must have lived together in peace and amity, without even a difference of opinion or desire". . .

The custom is said to have been instituted in the thirteenth century. The first reference to it is in *The Vision of Piers Plow-*

man, supposed to have been written by Robert Langlande about 1326 . . .

The oath taken is . . . recorded in the *Chartulary*:

"You shall swear, by custom of confession,
That you ne'er made nuptial transgression,
Nor since you were married man or wife,
By household brawls or contentious strife,
Or otherwise, in bed or at board,
Offended each other in deed or in word,
Or since the parish clerk said Amen,
Wished yourselves unmarried again,
Or in a Twelvemonth and a Day
Repented not in thought any manner of way,
But continued true in thought and desire
As when you joined hands in the Holy Quire."

Here it appears that the bacon was presented, and the following sentence pronounced:

"If to these conditions, without all fear
Of your own accord you freely swear
A whole gammon of bacon you shall receive
And bear it hence with love and good leave;
For this our custom of Dunmow, well known,
Though the cost be ours, the bacon's your own."

In 1869 advertisements appeared in the papers that claims might be sent in. A goodly number were forwarded, and two were selected —William Casson, wood engraver, and Emma Elizabeth, his wife . . . and Josiah Leaver, jeweller, and Mary Jane, his wife . . . They both received it on August 16th, and the festival was attended by twenty thousand persons. The next presentation was on August 10th, 1874 . . . Two years later, July 17th, 1876, the flitch was awarded to James Henry Boosey, parish clerk of Holy Trinity Church, Ventnor, Isle of Wight, and Mary his wife . . . This trial was presided over by the well-known antiquarian, Mr. William Andrews, of Hull, a frequent writer on historical subjects. In his introductory speech on this occasion, he traces the history of the custom, and adds the following: "You must, I think, all feel with me that the meeting to-day is well calculated to promote matrimonial happiness. We are the great rival of the divorce court. The name of Dunmow, and the remembrance of the flitch, causes the votaries of that court to hide in shame their heads. By the committee I am directed to state that they urge on claimants to remember that the prize must not be estimated by its cost, but by the distinction it offers to those who may be fortunate enough to obtain it. Enviable are the wedded pair on whom the prize is conferred, since the acquisition establishes a claim of honour and respect. To say that a couple ' deserve the flitch ' is a high compliment; but to say that ' they have actually won it ' is to proclaim them among the best and happiest of mankind."

From *Memorials of Old Essex*
Ed. by A. Clifton Kelway, 1908.

OF GOOD STOCK

THERE was lately residing at Stock, a boy, named Hills, the son of an industrious labourer, who had five grandfathers living. This extraordinary fact is thus explained: Farrow, who had a father living, married a young woman named Waldon, whose father was alive also, they had a daughter who married Hills, the father of the boy, who had a father and a grandfather living, thus Hills, sen., Hills, jun.; Farrow, sen., Farrow, jun., and Waldon, make the five. Their united ages amount to 332 years. I do not know whether the boy was favoured with a like supply of grandmothers.

From *Memorials of the Antiquities of . . . Essex*
by Alfred Suckling, 1845.

THE PRIDE OF THE FOREST

A . . . FAMOUS Essex revel centred upon Fairlop Oak. This huge old tree, which stood in Hainault Forest, had a girth of 36 feet. It was nearly 12 feet thick, and its seventeen branches, each as thick as an ordinary oak, spread their shade over an area 300 feet in circumference. Many a king and noble, and many a deerstealer too, many a robber, and many a simple peasant, must have sheltered beneath its branches during the long centuries in which it was the pride of the Forest.

Early in the eighteenth century, a worthy tradesman, who had made money in London, settled down in Essex, and conceived a great affection for the fine old tree. His name was Day; a curious, eccentric man, but so kind and generous that he generally went by the name of *Good Day*. This worthy man formed the custom of going, on the first Friday in every July, with some of his friends to Fairlop, and there eating, beneath his beloved oak, a dinner of beans and bacon. The fashion spread; from all the country round and from London too, folks came to eat their beans and bacon at Fairlop, and with them came pedlars and hawkers with all manner of trinkets for sale, showmen and tumblers and mountebanks of all kinds, and a great fair visited by thousands of people was set up.

A curious feature of the festival was the visit of some of Day's fellow tradesmen from Wapping. They came in a strange vehicle; a boat fashioned out of a single piece of wood mounted on wheels and drawn by six horses. Perhaps the form of the carriage was adopted as a compliment to one of the whims of the founder of the fair. He had a great dislike for land vehicles of all kinds. When he died and was carried, in a coffin made from a bough of the Fairlop Oak, to be buried in Barking Churchyard, his body was conveyed to the graveyard in a boat, in accordance with his dying request.

Fairlop Oak no longer stands. Careless people damaged it by fire in 1805, and some years afterwards the old tree, weakened by its injuries, was blown down in a great gale . . . At Lambourne End, we may still wander through a small but beautiful fragment of the once extensive Forest of Hainault in which the famous oak stood. Beyond the wood too, we may now walk over upland fields, once forest land, then turned into farms, and now made free to the people for ever.

From *School History of Essex*
by W. H. Weston, 1909.

THE LAWLESS COURT

A Court without justice, one can fancy a cynic saying, is nothing very remarkable, nor necessarily a feature of bygone days, but a lawless court is certainly unique; yet such a court, in name at any rate, the law-abiding county of Essex boasts.

This Lawless Court, or Court of Cockcrowing, is held annually at a spot known as King's Hill, in the Parish of Rochford, shortly after midnight on the Wednesday morning following Michaelmas Day.

At the appointed place of meeting stands a post, white-painted, about five feet high, to which the Steward of the Manor goes in procession from the King's Head Inn, with the tenants and torch-bearers; the company generally, assisted by any others who may be attracted by the singular ceremony, cockcrowing lustily. Arrived at the post, all at once become silent, while the steward or his deputy reads in a loud whisper the summons of the Court: " O yes! O yes! O yes! All manner of persons that do owe suit or service to this court, now to be holden in and for the Manor of King's Hill, in the Hundred of Rochford, draw near and give your attendance, and perform your several suits and services, according to the custom of the said manor. God save the Queen! " Then by the flickering light of the links, and in the same low voice, the roll is called of all persons owing service to the court, and of the lands in respect of which they owe it; answer being made by each tenant or his proxy in similar manner. The court is closed with another whispered proclamation; upon which, extinguishing their torches, and with a renewed outburst of cockcrowing, the company disperses.

From *Bygone Essex*
Edited by William Andrews, 1892.

OLD WIVES' TALES

THE Superstitions common among the labourers of Essex, though no doubt they are less firmly believed in than in the past, they are yet clung to, in many parts, with great tenacity. It rejoices the labourer's heart for instance if he meets a black cat, or a couple of crows, or even a man, as he goes to his work, for these apparitions mean good luck. But if he meets a female while going work-wards, it is strange to say, an evil omen. It is dangerous to kill a cat, to pass a person on the stairs, to rob certain nests, or to meet a snake or a weasel. A labourer's wife, if properly instructed in these matters, will not dare to weigh her infant before it is a year old, nor will she on any account cut its nails. A labourer will generally fear of disastrous consequences if he spills the salt, crosses knives or sticks, if he dreams of a tooth falling out, if he upsets a loaf in the oven, or unwittingly turns it upside down on the table, and he scrupulously avoids watching any person " out of sight," or stirring the leaves of the teapot with a spoon, a process which, he believes, stirs up trouble for himself. A rainy wedding he holds to be unlucky, but a rainy funeral is lucky. If strangers come on a Monday, there will be strangers all the week.

From *The Essex Labourer*
by W. Gurney Benham, 1888.

THE FINAL WORD

" A man of words and not of deeds,
Is like a garden full of weeds."

John Ray (1627-1705).

" A man, like a watch, is to be valued for his going.
He that prefers him on other accounts, bows to an idol."

William Penn (1644-1718).

" One must plough with the horses one has."

Charles Spurgeon (1834-1892).

" Men are known by little things, by the incidents of the day, better than they can be by more prominent and important events."

Stephen Morell.

" If you would enjoy true content, Live peacefully in that Vocation unto which Providence hath called you."

William Winstanley (1644-1703).

"... The genuine pleasures of life are elusive and seem to lie in the special occasions of commonplace amenities. They are the highlights, so to speak, of the ordinarily good."

Margery Allingham (1904-1966).

" Man is heaven's masterpiece ..."

Francis Quarles (1592-1644).

END NOTE

THE country is both the philosopher's garden and his library, in which he reads and contemplates the power, wisdom and goodness of God. It is his food as well as study; and gives him life, as well as learning.

From *Some Fruits of Solitude*
by William Penn (1644-1718).

THE reader must have perceived that with me Essex is a passion —almost a religion ... When ... I am bodily amidst the scenes I love, all else seems vain. I feel that I have come home ...

From *Romantic Essex*
by Reginald A. Beckett, 1901.